In the world of business and in the game of life, you usually find that the leader is an individual, male or female, who has mastered the skill of public oratory. Who are you going to follow? Someone who reads from a text? Or someone who speaks, without notes, from the heart? Pat Williams' *The Ultimate Handbook of Effective, Persuasive Speaking for Coaches and Leaders* is a must read for those who have a burning desire to lead others.

Harry Rhoads
Washington Speakers Bureau Co-CEO

Pat Williams' new book will help anyone who is in the speaking industry. Read his advice, put it into practice, and your communication skills will really take off.

Duane Ward
Premiere Speakers Bureau President

Pat Williams is a genius at effective communication! He knows it is a craft that must be constantly honed and polished to meet the ever-changing needs of an audience. This excellent book teaches you how to connect on a personal level in a variety of situations and styles.

Dr. Nido Qubein
High Point University President
Great Harvest Bread Company Chairman

Pat Williams is the only professional I know who is perfectly qualified to write this book. His sports background as an executive and his extensive experience as a big-time speaker makes this book a must have for any coach or leader.

Walter Bond ("Mr. Accountability")
Author and speaker

I love this book! It reminds me why I love the speaking industry. I am often asked by new speakers for advice on how to develop their careers. From now on, I will simply recommend Pat Williams' book.

Gail Davis
Gail Davis & Associates, Inc. President
International Association of Speakers Bureaus President

Pat Williams is one of the gems of the public speaking world. A terrific orator, a big man with a big heart and an important message. If you are looking to learn about effective speaking, you are learning from the master.

Jim Keppler
Keppler Speakers President

Pat Williams has written a public speaking book for the ages. The principles and advice on these pages will uplift any veteran speaker and help launch the careers of newcomers to the field. It's a winner.

Mark French
Leading Authorities President and CEO

The Ultimate Handbook of Effective, Persuasive Speaking for Coaches and Leaders

Pat Williams
with Jim Denney

COACHES
CHOICE™

ISBN: 978-1-60679-187-5
Library of Congress Control Number: 2011937190
Cover design: Studio J Art & Design
Book layout: Studio J Art & Design
Front cover photo: Brand X Pictures

Coaches Choice
P.O. Box 1828
Monterey, CA 93942
www.coacheschoice.com

Dedication

To Alfonso Castaneira, speech coach extraordinaire, who has had a profound influence on my speaking career.

Acknowledgments

With deep appreciation I acknowledge the support and guidance of the following people who helped make this book possible:

Special thanks to Bob Vander Weide, Rich DeVos, and Alex Martins of the Orlando Magic.

Hats off to my associate Andrew Herdliska; my proofreader, Ken Hussar; and my ace typist, Fran Thomas.

Thanks also to my writing partner, Jim Denney, for his superb contributions in shaping this manuscript.

Hearty thanks also go to the editorial team at Coaches Choice—including Angie Perry, Kristi Huelsing, and Jim Peterson—for believing that we had something important to say in these pages.

And, finally, special thanks and appreciation go to my wife, Ruth, and to my wonderful and supportive family. They are truly the backbone of my life.

Contents

1

A Reason to Speak

George Doyle

In the summer of 1963, after my second season as a catcher for the Philadelphia Phillies farm club in Miami, I said goodbye to my minor-league playing career and packed my belongings. I was bound for Indiana University in Bloomington to continue pursuit of my Master's degree in physical education. I called my mother, who lived in Wilmington, Delaware, and told her I'd come home for a week before going on to Indiana.

"I've got a better idea," Mom said. "Let's meet in Washington, D.C. Your sister and I are going to hear Dr. Martin Luther King, Jr. He's going to speak at the Lincoln Memorial on August 28."

That was my mom. She had been involved in social causes for as long as I could remember. Dr. King's legacy as a civil rights leader had been established during the Montgomery bus boycott in Alabama eight years earlier, but I was only vaguely aware of Dr. King at that time. As a young man, my life was consumed with sports, but I agreed to meet my mom and sister in D.C.

I drove from Miami to our nation's capital, and I'll always be grateful that my mother arranged for me to be in that vast crowd of 250,000 people for the March on Washington. It was one of the most incredible experiences of my life. Actors Charlton Heston, Marlon Brando, and Sidney Poitier lent star power to the event. Gospel music legend Mahalia Jackson sang "How I Got Over," Bob Dylan sang "Only a Pawn in Their Game," and Peter, Paul, and Mary sang "If I Had a Hammer" and "Blowin' In The Wind." On the National Mall, thousands of us stood shoulder-to-shoulder, ignoring the heat and humidity.

Finally, Dr. King got up to speak—and I became a witness to history and to Dr. King's "I Have a Dream" speech. Though I didn't understand the lasting significance of that speech, I recall being moved and stirred as Dr. King's words rolled over that crowd like thunder: "I still have a dream. It is a dream deeply rooted in the American Dream. I have a dream that one day this nation will rise up and live out the true meaning of its creed: 'We hold these truths to be self-evident, that all men are created equal.'"

It was not a long speech, just 17 minutes in length, yet those 17 minutes turned America in a new direction. Another man who was there that day, Congressman John Lewis of Georgia (then-president of the Student Non-Violent Coordinating Committee), recalled, "Dr. King had the power, the ability, and the capacity to transform those steps on the Lincoln Memorial into a monumental area that will forever be recognized. By speaking the way he did, he educated, he inspired, he informed not just the people there, but people throughout America and unborn generations."

I was surprised to learn that, while Dr. King spoke from a prepared text, some of the most memorable passages of that speech were actually improvised on the spot. At one point as he spoke, Mahalia Jackson called out to him, "Tell them about the dream, Martin!" Moments later, without missing a beat in that powerful cadence, he began describing his dream. If you watch the video of that speech, you see that when he begins the "I have a dream" passage, he stops glancing at his notes. Everything he says in the closing moments of that speech comes straight from his heart. He weaves together echoes from the Old Testament, the Declaration of Independence, the U.S. Constitution, Lincoln's Gettysburg Address and Emancipation Proclamation, and even Shakespeare's *Richard III*.

With the power of his words alone, Dr. King leveraged change in America. His "Dream" speech put pressure on the Kennedy administration and the Congress to act quickly on landmark civil rights legislation. Because of that speech, Dr. King was named *Time* magazine's "Man of the Year" in 1963. The following year, he was awarded the Nobel Peace Prize. Most important of all, Dr. King forced America to strive to live up to the promise of the Declaration of Independence and the Constitution—the promise of freedom, opportunity, and equality for all.

What is *your* dream? I know you have a dream. Everyone does.

You may dream of a successful career in coaching, corporate management, politics, religion, or the military. You may dream of changing the world or just one little corner of the world. Whatever your dream, you can achieve it if you know how to wield the power of the spoken word. Whenever you get up to speak in front of a group of people, you wield enormous power, more power than you realize. It's the power of persuasion, the power of motivation, the power of influence.

So think about your dream—then think about this: In the coming pages, you're going to learn how to achieve your dream through the power of spoken communication.

Why Speak?

"A lot of managers aren't bad at public speaking," business guru Tom Peters once said. "But 'not bad' ain't good enough."

You may say, "As a public speaker, I'm not bad. Not great, but not bad." Okay—but why stop at "not bad"? Why not reach for greatness? My goal in this book is to take you beyond the realm of "not bad," all the way to terrific!

And the place to start is with *your reason for speaking*. Before you give a speech, you need to know what your message is—and what you want your listeners to *do* about your message. You haven't come to simply dump information on people. You want to convince them, motivate them, move them to action, and change their lives.

So, at the outset, you have to ask yourself, "What is my message? And what qualifies me to speak on this theme? Why should 50 or a 100 or 1,000 or 10,000 people sit quietly and listen to me talk?" The answer to that question is the first vital element of any speech.

I have heard one guesstimate that there are as many as 100,000 speeches given every day in America. That's a lot of verbiage! In fact, I suspect the actual number is even higher. Imagine all the speeches given in all the cities and towns across America:

- The many pep talks and motivational speeches given by coaches in every sport, before practices, meets, and games, at every level, professional, scholastic, and amateur
- All the talks given at Rotary Clubs, Kiwanis Clubs, Lions Clubs, and other civic organizations across the country
- The sales reports, business presentations, product rollouts, and boardroom talks delivered in corporate meeting rooms across this land
- The political speeches and presentations given at every level, from the local school board or planning commission to the President's State of the Union address
- The sermons, homilies, invocations, wedding messages, and eulogies given by clergy every day of the week
- All the lectures and discourses delivered by professors to college and university students on campuses around the country

And the list goes on and on. I would be surprised if there were *only* 100,000 speeches being given every day across the United States. I think the number must be easily five or 10 times that. Whatever the actual number is, we can be sure of one thing: There are *a lot* of verbs, nouns, and adjectives being tossed into the air every day.

But how much of all that "speechifying" is really fascinating, motivating, persuasive, and worthwhile to an audience? How much of that torrent of communication actually results in action and change? How many of the hundreds of thousands of speeches that are spoken every day are of such high caliber that you would set aside an hour of your life and give that speaker your undivided attention?

I truly believe that we would change the way we communicate if we would remember that public speaking is not about the speaker—it's about the audience. What does the audience *need* to hear? What do your listeners *want* to hear? What are their hurts and fears—and how can you, the speaker, helped to heal those hurts and calm those fears? The audience hasn't come to serve you. Rather, you, the speaker, must serve the needs of the audience.

Sportscaster Dick Enberg once told me, "Know your audience, and relate your speech to their needs. Find out what their concerns are, and speak to those concerns." And Jack Canfield, author, speaker, and cofounder of the *Chicken Soup for the Soul* publishing phenomenon, once told me how he approaches every audience at every event at which he speaks: "Love your audience," he said. "You are there with a sense of purpose because you want to give them a gift. If you're there for yourself, they will pick up on that. If you're there for *them*, they will know that as well."

That's a transformative insight: Know your audience. Love your audience. Give your audience a gift—the gift of your insight, your caring, your message. Business speaker Tom Peters once explained it to me this way: "The best speakers are literally converting one individual at a time. If there are 5,000 people in your audience, you are still looking at them as individuals. You become one of them, and you genuinely feel their pain. You've got to care about them. You've got to be real and disclose who you are as an authentic human being. Be totally vulnerable. People can sense that a mile away."

I know you have a message, a reason to speak, and you want to communicate that message as effectively and persuasively as possible. That's why you're reading this book. So let's jump right in and get down to the brass tacks of becoming a great public speaker.

Your "Signature Speech"

If you want to become an effective speaker, my first piece of advice to you is this: *perfect one message*. Sit down and craft one speech that expresses the core passion of your life. Hone it, practice it, nail it to the wall, make it 100 percent yours. That message should be unique to you, a speech no one else but you could deliver. It should be full of fresh, compelling ideas that your audience has never heard before, ideas that will impact your listeners at a deep level. Practice it until you could deliver it in your sleep. I call that a "signature speech."

Later, you can come up with additional talks on related subjects. You can master them and polish them to that same degree. But at the beginning of your speaking career, make sure you have one message, your ace in the hole that you can always pull out on a moment's notice. All great speakers have their go-to message, their signature speech, ready for any eventuality.

A great signature speech should be long enough to fill at least 40 to 50 minutes— yet it should be flexible enough so that you can edit on the fly and deliver the essence of that speech in as little as 15 or 20 minutes. Let me list for you a few successful professional speakers from various walks of life, along with their signature speeches. I think you'll be able to identify with at least one and maybe several of these speakers:

- Tony Dungy is the former head coach of the 2007 Super Bowl champion Indianapolis Colts. His signature speech is called "Leading Successful Teams," in which he talks about setting goals, being disciplined, maintaining integrity, and overcoming adversity as the keys to successful teams.
- Jerry Linenger is a former NASA astronaut who flew aboard both the American space shuttle and the Russian space station *Mir*. During his 132 days aboard Mir, the space station suffered a series of emergencies—a life-threatening fire, a loss of altitude control (causing the space station to tumble in orbit), failure of the onboard life-support systems, and a near collision with a cargo ship. Out of these adventures

came Linenger's signature speech, "Challenges and Change: My 132 Days Off the Planet," a motivational talk about how to summon courage and tap into personal resources to overcome obstacles and achieve success.

- Claire Shipman is a correspondent with ABC News. Her signature speech is called "Womenomics: Write Your Own Rules for Success," and is aimed at helping working women take charge of their careers in the current economy.

- General Peter Pace, USMC (Ret.) served as chairman of the Joint Chiefs of Staff from 2005 to 2007. His signature speech, "We All Answer to Someone: Leadership Up and Down," presents his unique viewpoint on leadership, including the ethical responsibilities of being a leader, the need for followers to respect leaders, and for leaders to set a good example for followers.

- Terry Bradshaw, legendary Steelers quarterback and sports broadcaster, communicates with homespun humor and fascinating stories as he delivers his signature speech, "Why Not Your Best?" With an engaging and entertaining style, he delivers strategies for continual self-improvement and competitiveness.

- Debbi Fields is an entrepreneur and the founder of Mrs. Fields Cookies. Her signature speech, "Her First Secret Recipe: Making It Against All Odds," is a message only Mrs. Fields could give, drawn from her experiences as the founder of the most successful cookie empire in the world. She talks about excellence, perseverance, and remaining true to yourself as the keys to reaching the top.

- Basketball analyst Dick Vitale is the essence of energy, enthusiasm, and motivation. His signature speech is "The Game of Life," a message of optimism and life lessons, delivered with inimitable Vitale vitality.

- Heather Whitestone McCallum, the first hearing-impaired Miss America, has a signature talk called "Spiritual Beauty" about facing life's challenges with faith and courage, based on her own experiences and the Old Testament story of Queen Esther.

- Former Reagan administration official and talk show host William Bennett has a signature speech called "Mornings in America," which analyzes politics, culture, and education issues in light of Reaganesque conservative values.

- Political commentator Mark Shields has worked for Robert F. Kennedy, Ed Muskie, and Sargent Shriver. He brings a wealth of stories and insider insights to his signature talk, "The Wit and Wisdom of Mark Shields."

- Sally Ride, America's first woman in space, brings "the right stuff" to her signature talk, "Reach for the Stars." She recalls her experiences in the male-dominated NASA program and her two flights aboard the space shuttle *Challenger*, while imparting her insights regarding the key ingredients for success and leadership.

- NASCAR driver Kyle Petty tells exciting stories about life in the fast lane—and life in the pits—in his signature talk, "What a Ride: Life, Family, Community, and the Race Track." He talks about the Petty family values, which have brought fame and success to his clan for three generations.

- Ann Rhoades, a former JetBlue top executive, brings her unique people-centric belief system to her signature talk, "Built on Values: Creating an Enviable Culture That Outperforms the Competition."
- Duke University men's basketball coach Mike Krzyzewski shares how the life lessons he learned from his parents, his West Point education, and his coaching career have taken him to pinnacle of his profession. His signature talk is called "Victory Through Teamwork and Leadership."
- Dr. Benjamin Carson is a renowned pediatric surgeon and a great speaker and storyteller. In his signature speech, "Think Big," Dr. Carson recounts his incredible journey from a troubled inner-city youth to one of the most highly regarded surgeons in the world. It's an inspiring speech about personal excellence and our influence on others.

Now, in saying that each of these speakers has a "signature speech," I'm not saying they can only sing one note or only give one speech. Most of them have an impressive repertoire of speeches. But each of them has that *one* speech that he or she can call upon in any situation, on demand, and at a moment's notice. That speech defines them. They can deliver it without notes. They can improvise. They can motivate and move an audience with that one go-to speech. That's why it's their *signature* speech.

What is *your* signature message? What are you passionate about? What do you love to talk about? What theme or cause or message *defines* you?

"I don't know what to say!"

Many times in my 40-odd years of speaking, I was called upon to give an impromptu talk. Having a signature speech to fall back on has saved my neck more times than I can count.

Every so often, I'm sitting in an audience, and the person on the podium will look out over the crowd and say, "Oh! I see Pat Williams is here! Pat, would you like to come up here and say a few words? Come on up!"

What can I do? Everyone is waiting for me to go up and speak—so I go up and speak! As I'm walking to the podium, people applaud and expect to hear inspiring thoughts pouring from my voice box. So I think quickly, my synapses firing furiously, and I ask myself, "What do I say?"

Then I remember my signature speech.

If they want me to talk for five minutes, no problem! I can slug out a five-minute excerpt from my patented speech, and plug it right into that time slot. If they need 15, 20, 30 minutes, I have it right between my ears, ready to go.

When you have that one well-honed speech—a talk you've given dozens or hundreds of times—you are never at a loss for words. You don't have it memorized word for word. Instead, you've got the content organized in your mind. You know where this story goes, where to fit in that quotation. You can juggle it around a bit, and no one in your audience will know the difference. Best of all, you'll always come off looking calm, articulate, and totally in charge.

You never have to feel uncomfortable on a stage, you never worry about cold sweat again. Whenever anyone taps you to "come on up and say a few words," you can tell yourself, "Hey, I've got nothing to worry about. I've got the perfect little speech tucked away in my brain."

Usually, if someone wants you to speak impromptu, they'll give you at least a few minutes to gather your thoughts: "Would you mind saying a few words after dessert?" That will give you time to jot down a little outline on a napkin or mentally run through your go-to speech. And that's all the time you'll need.

The great thing about those "impromptu" remarks is that, while you may *appear* to be sharing off the top of your head, you will know (and *no one* but you will know) that these thoughts are actually very well thought out remarks. You have already taken the time to master your talk, to break it down into bite-sized bits, ready to be delivered anytime—and you'll look like a pro.

Anytime you get up to speak, whether your presentation has been booked months in advance or moments in advance, your assignment is to stand up before a roomful of strangers and win them over. And you can do that if you have a signature speech.

Nothing is more rewarding than to finish a speech and then receive the enthusiastic ovation that says, "Wow! We're impressed! You have touched us! You have moved us! You have motivated us!" There is no greater experience a speaker can have than when people come up afterward and say, "You said *exactly* what I needed to hear." There's no more heady feeling in the world than to receive that kind of feedback and appreciation from an audience.

While I was working on this book, Michael Reagan came on my Orlando radio show to promote his book, *The New Reagan Revolution*. He shared with me the story of his father, Ronald Reagan, at the 1976 Republican National Convention. Reagan, the former California governor, had waged a hard-fought primary against incumbent President Gerald Ford. Reagan garnered more votes, but Ford won more delegates. Governor Reagan hoped to score an upset at the convention and wrest the nomination away from the sitting Republican president, but to no avail.

On the final night of the convention, President Ford gave his acceptance speech before the delegates—then he did something totally unprecedented. He beckoned to the skybox where his defeated rival, Ronald Reagan, sat with his wife, Nancy. "Ron," said Ford, "would you come down and bring Nancy?"

So the Reagans left the skybox as the band played "California, Here I Come." When they joined Gerald and Betty Ford on the platform, Governor Reagan leaned over to Nancy and whispered, "I don't know what to say."

Moments later, Ronald Reagan stepped up to the microphone and gave a five-minute speech that stunned everyone on the convention floor. It was a speech about Reagan's love for his country and his concern about America's future. It was, by turns, eloquent, wistful, challenging, and electrifying. The delegates were awed. Some wept. Michael told me that, when his father finished speaking, many delegates were thinking, "We've nominated the wrong man!"

That powerful five-minute speech laid the groundwork for Ronald Reagan's triumphant return to the national stage four years later, when he was elected President of the United States. Even though Reagan had said, "I don't know what to say," he was not at a loss for words. In fact, he delivered some of the most important words of his career. How was he able to come up with a brilliant, well-structured, persuasive speech on the spur of the moment?

Answer: He had plenty of go-to material to draw upon. Even before he was governor of California, Ronald Reagan had spent 10 years as spokesman for General Electric, touring the country by train and giving as many as a dozen speeches per day. He had *scores* of signature speeches that he could reformat in many ways. Michael told me he had seen the 3x5 cards his father had written in his own hand. In fact, Ronald Reagan would sometimes shuffle his note cards "just to make things interesting." Reagan's General Electric years had given him the best training a communicator could have.

That's why—as Michael Reagan said on my show—Ronald Reagan "was not just the Commander in Chief. He was also the Communicator in Chief."

I once interviewed speech coach Aram Bakshian, Jr., who was director of speechwriting in the Reagan White House. I asked Aram to name the qualities that earned Ronald Reagan the title "the Great Communicator." He said, "President Reagan had a strong, clear message, and he didn't get distracted. There was a definite conviction to his message, which he could project to an audience. He always sought common ground with his audience. Mr. Reagan was a genuine person, and people identified with that."

Now that you know his secret, you can go and do likewise. Craft your signature speech, and keep it clear, simple, and uncomplicated. Practice it, learn it, own it, and deliver it wherever and whenever you can. Once you have mastered your signature speech, you will be ready at a moment's notice to give the presentation of a lifetime.

A Message That Defines You

In an essay called "The Scaffolding of Rhetoric," Sir Winston Churchill wrote, "Of all the talents bestowed upon men, none is more precious than the gift of oratory. He who enjoys it wields a power more durable than that of a great king. He is an independent force in the world. Abandoned by his party, betrayed by his friends, stripped of his offices, whoever can command this power is still formidable."[1]

Leadership generally gravitates to the man or woman who can talk, who can stand up in front of people and express ideas and goals in a way that persuades and motivates. The compelling speaker is usually the one who gets the accolades and promotions, the one we elect to office, the one who gets the leadership job, the executive position, the head coaching job.

The power to move people with words alone is one of the greatest of all powers. When you communicate to an audience, you transfer your insight, your enthusiasm, and your passion to your audience. You persuade them to embrace your cause. You wield enormous influence. And the key to that influence is having a reason for your speech, a message that you own, a message that defines you.

I developed my own signature speech early in my career. I first began taking speaking opportunities in my 20s and early 30s when I was a young baseball executive in the Phillies farm system. Before long, I moved on to executive positions with the Philadelphia 76ers and the Chicago Bulls, and was frequently called upon to speak at various events. Those speaking opportunities gave me a chance to promote the team, and I was eager to take every opportunity.

Winning and leadership were the themes that ignited my passion. So I decided to develop one well-organized, highly focused talk on those themes. I read a book by the Reverend Bob Richards, the "Vaulting Vicar," who gained fame in the 1940s and '50s as an Olympic pole vaulter and decathlete. His motivational book, *The Heart of a Champion*, was like an elixir to my soul. I devoured its principles, then composed my own signature talk about the attitude and actions that set winners apart.

I crafted that talk, then practiced and honed it until I owned it. I have delivered versions of that talk at least a thousand times over my career. To this very day, my talk "Finding the Will to Win," which contains echoes of that early signature speech, remains one of my most requested talks. I now have many talks in my speaker's repertoire, but my earliest signature speech, crafted more than 40 years ago, still stands me in good stead today.

After I had been speaking for several years, I knew it was time to craft a second signature speech. I was getting repeat invitations, and I knew I couldn't give an audience the same speech two years in a row. I had recently read a book by longtime NFL great

Bill Glass, in which he talked about building a ladder to your dreams. Bill is a good friend, and with his help and inspiration, I crafted a speech about reaching our dreams. Echoes of that speech can still be heard in my speeches today.

Where do you find material for a great speech? Well, you find material anywhere and everywhere. It's just a matter of keeping your eyes open and noticing what's happening around you.

There are speech ideas and stories in your everyday life. You find them all around you—in your family, in the things your children say, in the interesting things people do at work, in the stories you see on TV or hear on the radio or read in books and newspapers. You find ideas and stories in the great events or little human interest stories you read about, and in biographies of famous people.

Soon after our family moved to Orlando, I was flipping through *Reader's Digest*, and I came upon an article about Walt Disney's five secrets of success. I learned that Orlando was a sleepy little town in central Florida before Walt built his theme park here. Walt Disney completely transformed this region. So, from the time I arrived here, I wanted to know everything there was to know about Walt Disney. That little article was a life-changer for me.

I began devouring books on Walt Disney. The Disney magic began seeping into my thinking, then into my speaking, then into my writing. I ended up writing a book about Walt's success secrets, *Go for the Magic*, and a few years later, I followed that up with another book, *How to Be Like Walt*. Out of my love for Walt Disney and my enthusiasm for his success principles, I have crafted a speech that teaches his five secrets of success. You never know where a life-changing talk may be lurking. It might even be waiting for you in the pages of *Reader's Digest*.

When I became immersed in the speaking world in Orlando, I received repeated requests for two topics: leadership and teamwork. These topics were requested especially by organizations and event planners in the corporate world. I had touched on these subjects in my speaking for a number of years, but as the demand for these topics accelerated, I knew I had to respond to this demand. I knew I had an urgent reason to speak, specifically and in-depth, on these two subjects. So I quickly organized my leadership and teamwork talks so that I could deliver them in any setting, at any time.

The first lesson of becoming a great public speaker is to ask yourself, "What is my reason to speak?" Craft a speech around that reason. Focus it. Own it. Hone it to a crystal-clear, diamond-hard edge. Then deliver it again and again, at every opportunity. Once you have a reason to speak, a whole new world will open up for you.

Next, let's see how to organize your message and create your signature speech.

2

Getting Organized

Hemera/Thinkstock

After giving literally thousands of speeches in my career, I'm amazed to look back to my ninth grade year in Miss Barbara Bullard's English class. Miss Bullard allowed each student one 3x5 note card for a three-minute speech. I wrote my entire speech, word for word, in lettering so tiny I would have needed a jeweler's loupe to read it.

The day I was to deliver my speech, I sat at my desk, dreading the moment Miss Bullard would call my name. When she finally said, "Patrick," I got to my feet, made my way to the front of the room, peered down at the little index card in my sweaty palm—and couldn't read a single word! My heart hammered in my chest. My knees knocked like castanets. My voice sounded like a Swiss yodeler as I stammered my way through my pitiful little speech.

Somewhere around the middle of my speech, the tiny print just seemed to blur before my eyes. I lost my place and couldn't pick up the next line. I was frozen, petrified—and I just stopped and stood there, completely lost. You can imagine the reaction of the class. My classmates were embarrassed for me, looking down at their desks. Finally, I slunk back to my own desk and sat down, dejected and defeated.

Needless to say, my first attempt at oratory was an unmitigated disaster. It's a wonder I ever summoned the nerve to stand before an audience again! In fact, I might have ended my speaking career forever right then and there if Miss Bullard hadn't called me to her desk after class. She encouraged me, gave me a pep talk, told me I could master this skill. "Let's work on this together," she said. "Let me show you a better note system." I eventually got through her class with a C-minus.

During my junior year at Wake Forest University, something happened that finally pulled me out of my shell of insecurity and shyness. I don't know what caused the transformation, but I think it had something to do with my boyhood admiration for radio sports announcers. I had often daydreamed of being a sports announcer myself. Finally, I went to the campus radio station and asked Dr. Julian Burroughs, the station manager, for the opportunity to sit behind the microphone. He assigned me the job of broadcasting freshman basketball games and hosting a sports interview show.

Dr. Burroughs gave me the freedom to design my own format, choose the theme music, book the guests, and write the interview questions. Sometimes, I conducted interviews in the studio, and sometimes I lugged a heavy reel-to-reel tape recorder around and recorded interviews on location. I got to interview some big names—from my baseball idol Ted Williams to golfing great Arnold Palmer to evangelist Billy Graham. In the process, I discovered that if I took on a challenge that scared me, and I conquered it, my confidence soared—and I had *fun*.

The experience boosted my confidence as a public speaker. I continued to take speech classes, and the skills I acquired have served me well to this day.

Organization and Preparation Are Vital

I've always had a fascination with the spoken word.

Because Orlando is a convention destination, almost every major speaker in the world passes through these portals at some point. When I have the opportunity, I love to hear them speak, especially the sports figures. Some of the top names in sports are out on the speaking circuit, and I've had the privilege of hearing most of them. Many are friends of mine.

But sports speakers often leave me frustrated. They'll speak for an hour while I sit there with my yellow legal pad, my pen poised, ready to take notes—but I can't! Their talks do not lend themselves to note-taking.

Sports guys are often engaging storytellers, but their talks are often haphazardly structured. They tell a lot of anecdotes, but those stories do not connect to a theme, to any point they are making. The audience is entertained for a while by a sports hero—but their lives have not been changed, their thinking has not been challenged. They come away without any insights or principles they can use in their daily lives.

Whenever I listen to one of these speakers, I think, "I'd love to sit down for 30 minutes with you, sir, and go into detail about how to take your speech from ordinary to great. Not only would it enhance the experience of your audience, but it just might transform *your* life as well."

There are many retired athletes from various sports who would have a lot to offer on the convention and corporate lecture circuit. They could command five-figure speaking fees—but what are they doing? They're earning a fraction of that, signing autographs at sports memorabilia shows. Nothing wrong with that—but why not take their game to the next level? Why not share the *real* wisdom they have to offer? Why not organize their stories and ideas into a presentation that would change lives—including their own?

It's essentially a matter of organization, planning, and preparation. The only confident, influential speaker is a *prepared* speaker. Organization and preparation are vital to your success as a communicator. As author and pastor Mark Atteberry told me, "Preparation is crucial to public speaking. You've got to do your homework. Always assume that there will be someone in the audience who knows more about your topic than you do."

My friend Ken Hussar put it this way: "Be organized. If you're going nowhere, any road will take you there. But if you want your hearers to travel with you, you need a clear, uncluttered route. Great speakers are able to distill hundreds of hours of preparation and years of real-life experience into three or four vital points that listeners can take with them and put into practice."

Preparing for a speech does not have to consume your life and your schedule. In fact, the best way to prepare for a speech is to work at it a little bit each day, not cram for it all at once. Select a topic that you know and can speak about with energy and passion. As you develop your talk, practice delivering different pieces of it. See how it flows. See how the different sections fit together. See if the stories work well. Experiment with your talk. Edit out material that doesn't work, and replace it with new and better material. As you prepare your material, let your speech find its own natural rhythms, structure, and pace.

As you practice your speech, you'll come to know it intimately, inside and out, backward and forward. Your confidence will grow. You'll become more and more confident and comfortable with the idea of delivering your speech without notes. You'll like the idea of standing in front of your audience without the barrier of a lectern. You'll feel your confidence grow as you realize you don't have to deliver a word-for-word script. You can actually have a *conversation* with your audience.

That kind of confidence comes from organization and preparation.

The Structure of Your Speech

One of the highest compliments I ever receive as a speaker is when someone comes up to me after my talk and says, "Look at my notebook! I filled pages with notes from your speech!" When I see that notebook, I know that my words didn't just float away on the air; they impacted lives. The influence I have on others is the reason I'm a public speaker today.

I have found that the way to organize a speech for impact is to "do it by the numbers." Once you know what your message is, once you have a reason to speak, it helps to break your message down into numbered points. That's why my speeches have titles like "Walt Disney's Five Secrets of Success" or "The Seven Sides of Leadership Excellence" or "The Eight Qualities of Outstanding Teams." When I begin speaking, the audience members are on notice that my talk will follow a logical, numerical sequence. They can get organized to take notes.

The mark of an effective speech is a logical structure that the audience can follow. As you craft your speech, ask yourself: "Can my listeners take this material right now, absorb it, and put it immediately into action in their lives and careers?" If the answer is yes, then you have created an effective speech that will truly impact and influence your listeners.

Start with the main theme of your speech, your reason for speaking. This is your bottom line, your takeaway, the big idea you want the people in your audience to have fixed in their minds by the end of your talk.

Divide that theme into three or more sub-themes or supporting points. For example, when I speak on "The Seven Sides of Leadership Excellence," I start with a main theme of "leadership excellence," which I divide into seven sub-themes: vision, communication, people skills, character, competence, boldness, and a servant's heart. I have at least one or two stories to illustrate each of those seven leadership principles or supporting points.

Once your speech is organized, you know exactly where your speech is going. You can see the entire structure of your talk at a glance. This helps you to fix the outline of your speech in your mind. You can visualize it, like a roadmap in your mind, so that you know exactly where you are at all times. Once you have your main theme divided into sub-themes, you can plug stories into each of those sub-themes.

For example, in my leadership talk, I have one or two stories that illustrate what it means to be a leader of vision, then a story or two about being a leader who has good communication skills, then a story or two about demonstrating good people skills, and so on. Each story should be locked in tightly on each principal, so that every story helps the audience understand that principal more clearly. We don't want a people skills story floating around in the vision section of the speech. We want to enlighten our listeners, not confuse them.

The audience wants to follow you and keep up with you, so be a good tour guide. Let your audience know exactly where you've been, where you are, and where you're going. Don't leave them in the wilderness.

People who are just starting out as public speakers often ask me, "What about notes? Is it okay to speak from notes?" Yes. When you're starting out in your speaking career, notes can be very helpful. But notes can also become a crutch. Your ultimate goal is to free yourself of the need to continually refer to notes.

The worst thing you can do as a speaker is to write your speech out like a script, sentence by sentence, then read it to your audience. People didn't come to hear you read to them. They came to hear you speak from your heart.

If you must use notes, keep them brief. At most, use a few trigger words to jog your memory, a two- or three-word phrase, or a symbol or doodle. For example, suppose in my "Leadership" speech, I have a note card which reads:

Vision 3 effects	*1—Focus*
2—Fuel	*3—Finish*

Now, those are sparse notes—but with a little practice, you could speak for five to 10 minutes from that one note card. These notes tell us that the leadership quality of vision produces three effects. Those three effects are *focus*, *fuel*, and the ability to *finish* what you start. You don't want to have your entire speech written out in sentence form. You merely want your notes to trigger the thoughts and ideas that are already stored in your memory. Those triggers will enable you to form your sentences on the fly, just as you would in a one-on-one conversation. If I were speaking from that note card, I would say something like this:

"Vision produces three important effects in the life of an effective leader:

"First, your vision keeps you focused on your goal. A vision of the future draws you forward and keeps you from wandering off onto rabbit trails and detours.

"Second, your vision is fuel for your journey. It's your source of energy and enthusiasm for all the challenges you will face as a leader. Vision fuels your passion, and passion is the most contagious of all human qualities. If you want to measure the temperature of any organization, just stick a thermometer in the leader's mouth! When a leader is energized and enthusiastic, that passion radiates throughout the organization! And that kind of passion is fueled by vision.

"Third, your vision enables you to finish strong. A leadership role is a tough challenge. The road ahead is bumpy. You have mountains to climb and deserts to cross that you can't even imagine right now. How will you keep going when the going gets tough? You keep going because you have a vision of a bright and shining future leading you on, pulling you forward, motivating you to persevere, driving you to finish."

Now, I could go on and on. I could tell stories from my own leadership experience, or I could tell stories about great leaders of the past, from Washington to Walt Disney, and show how their vision of the future enabled them to stay focused, stay fueled, and finish strong. But you get the point. All you need is a few trigger words at most to remind you of what you came to say. A glance at those trigger words on your notes will crack open the shell of your memory and all of those ideas, insights, and stories will come tumbling out.

As you speak, not reading from a script but actually conversing with your audience, engaging them with your eyes, receiving their feedback as they smile back at you and nod and acknowledge the great points you're making—you'll be brilliant! You'll be amazing! You'll make a connection with your audience, and they'll think, "Wow! The speaker is actually talking to *me*!"

Eventually, you're going to be able to deliver a polished, professional speech without any notes at all. We'll talk about that later. But at the beginning, there's nothing wrong with a few simple notes to prod your memory so that you can follow the outline of your speech.

As you organize and craft your speech, remember that you're not giving a speech merely to dump information on your audience. You are there to motivate your audience to action. So, above all, give the people in your audience action steps that they can apply to their lives immediately. Your speech should be persuasive, energizing, and motivating. When people listen to you speak, they should want to get up, rush out, and accomplish great things. So get them excited, get them pumped up, and then give them work to do.

If your speeches don't change people's lives and motivate people to action, why speak?

The Key to Confidence

According to *The Book of Lists* by David Wallechinsky and Amy Wallace, the worst fear that plagues most people is the fear of public speaking—that's the number-one fear on the list! Amazingly, the fear of death comes in at number seven. That's why Jerry Seinfeld once said, "This means to the average person, if you go to a funeral, you're better off in the casket than doing the eulogy."

But I am here to testify that it is possible to overcome your fear of public speaking. In fact, you can become a confident speaker, a poised speaker, a speaker who is always in command of the situation. The key to confidence in public speaking is to be a prepared and organized speaker.

Permit me to make a bold statement: The speaker who needs notes has no right to be confident. That speaker *should* be nervous.

You're probably thinking, "But how can I give a speech without notes? How am I supposed to remember what I came to say? If I get up in front of people without notes, I'll get so flustered I won't remember my name, much less my speech. What am I supposed to do, memorize my speech word for word?"

Absolutely not! When you get up to speak, the audience doesn't want to hear you give a recitation that you've learned by rote. The people in that audience want to know that you're a real person, and that you've come to communicate to them with your heart, your soul, and your passion. As sportscaster Dick Enberg once told me, "Don't memorize your speech, and don't read to people, either. Make your speech as spontaneous as possible."

Passion doesn't come from memorization. You can't squeeze heart and soul from a stack of 3x5 cards. All the ingredients of a great communicator must come from *inside of you*. When you have your message prepared and organized, when you have practiced giving your talk dozens of times, you won't know it word for word, but you'll *feel* it deep inside. You'll have the structure and shape of your message lodged between your ears. You'll have the passion and energy of your message burning in your soul. You'll have all of the stories and principles and insights of your message right on the tip of your tongue.

Ultimately, you'll gain the confidence to leave the safety and security of your notes and your lectern. You'll possess the confidence to launch out and deliver an entire 30-, 45-, or even a 60-minute speech without notes *and* without fear.

The prepared and organized speaker is one who can put a talk together in logical order, and then practice it until it is second nature. That speaker can get up before an audience knowing, "I am ready for this. I know what I came here to say, I have it locked down. I'm not nervous or scared. I don't have time to be nervous. I'm ready. Let's do this."

I believe there's a progression to a person's growth as a public speaker. This has certainly been the progression of my career. In my conversations with other professional speakers, I find that almost all of them have gone through the same progression.

Step One: No Confidence. You have your speech written out word for word, line by line. Hands shaking, knees knocking, you approach the lectern with a stack of papers in hand—more of a manuscript than speech notes. Standing behind the lectern, clutching your papers, you deliver the speech exactly as written, desperately glancing up from time to time so that it doesn't look so much like you're reading. You try to read with some expression in your voice, but you make no connection with the audience—and the people in the audience seem restless, uncomfortable, and maybe even embarrassed for you. They sense your fear and insecurity.

Step Two: Clutching the Security Blanket. You replace the fully written speech with note cards. You're still behind the lectern, clinging to that barrier for a small sense of security. The speech on your note cards isn't written out word for word, but you fear you might forget something, so your stories, transitions, and major points are spelled out. You make better eye contact now that you're not reading your speech, but you still lack the confidence of a great speaker. You are clutching the security blanket of the lectern and your notes.

Step Three: Taking Baby Steps. Your confidence is growing. You still have your notes, you're still behind the lectern. But now you feel confident enough to move about on the stage, to take some baby steps away from the lectern from time to time. You know your material well enough that the notes aren't really necessary—but you keep them close in case you panic. It's starting to dawn on you that the lectern is really getting in the way of a connection between you and your audience. You're making progress—but only baby steps so far. You know you want to get closer to your audience, but you're not ready to take that *big* step of leaving your notes behind.

Step Four: Time to Solo. This is huge. This is a momentous turning point in your speaking career. You are ready to abandon the support and security of the lectern. You are ready to spread your wings and fly. So you step away from the lectern, you come down the steps from the stage, and you are now on the floor in front of the first row, addressing your audience eye to eye. You may still have a couple of note cards in your hand, but you have broken down the wall between you and your audience. It's an exhilarating feeling the first time you do that. There is nothing between you and the audience—and believe me, you now have their full attention. You'll see the people in your audience sit upright in their seats and lean expectantly forward. You've got them in the palm of your hand.

But there is still one more step to take—and it's a biggie.

Step Five: Total Freedom! You have given up your notes. You have left the safety and security of the lectern. You have erased all barriers between you and your audience. Now you actually walk out into the audience. You move freely up the aisle or among the tables. You shake hands, pat people on the shoulders, read their name tags and call them by name. No longer are you on a platform above them. You are experiencing a level of speaker-audience intimacy that you never would have dreamed possible before.

I have another name for this step in your progress as a public speaker. I call it "The Elizabeth Dole Stroll." You may remember Elizabeth Dole as the wife of presidential candidate Robert Dole, who ran against incumbent Bill Clinton in 1996. At the Republican National Convention, she gave a speech called "Why I Love Bob"—a speech that told the story of her husband's life, from Senator Dole's childhood in Kansas to his service in World War II to his career in Washington, D.C. Elizabeth Dole's speech stunned and electrified the nation—not so much because of what she said but because of how she said it.

During that 20-minute speech, delivered entirely without notes, Elizabeth Dole walked around the floor at eye-level with her audience. She approached audience members, walked among them, and touched them. The looks on their faces showed that they loved her—and they were awed by her.

She stood in front of women in the crowd and talked about all that Bob Dole had done to help women in the workplace. She'd describe her husband as "the strongest and the most compassionate, most tender man I've ever known … my own personal Rock of Gibraltar," and the TV camera caught tears glinting in the eyes of her listeners. With her sunny Southern charm, she talked about her husband's accomplishments, then asked, "I think that's a pretty good record, don't you?" And the audience smiled back and nodded vigorously.

That speech gave Bob Dole a big bounce in the polls. The media dubbed it "The Talk Show Speech" and compared Elizabeth Dole to Oprah Winfrey. Her speech was so successful that the campaign gave her a staff of 30 and sent her out to campaign separately for the Bob Dole-Jack Kemp ticket. Though Bob Dole was defeated in the November election, Elizabeth Dole's strolling speech at the convention became a defining moment in her career, and is credited as a big factor in her election as North Carolina's first female senator in November 2002.

No Security in Security Blankets

One of the great ironies of public speaking is that the more we cling to our security blankets, the less secure and successful we become. We tend to think, "If I have a script that I can read line for line, I won't get lost, I won't forget what to say, and I won't look stupid in front of an audience." Nothing could be farther from the truth.

In August 2005, Jeanine Pirro, the Republican district attorney of Westchester County, New York, announced that she was running for the United States Senate. She made her announcement at a press conference at the Waldorf Astoria. Her speech was printed out word for word on typing paper, and about halfway through the speech she simply stopped and stared at her notes. A page of her speech was missing. While members of the media shifted uncomfortably and murmured among themselves, Pirro riffled through her stack of pages. Cameras flashed as she leaned to a staffer and asked, "Do you have a page 10?" Finally, after an embarrassing 32-second lapse, she went on with the rest of her speech.

Soon after Pirro's troubled press conference, the chairman of the state Democratic Party told reporters, "The speech was long on attacks and literally silent on specifics for New Yorkers—32 seconds of silence that spoke volumes."[1] Just two months after entering the race, Pirro withdrew. Many pundits point to her stumbling performance while announcing her candidacy as the reason she was never able to gain the confidence of voters and the support of donors.

The media-age equivalent of a typed speech script is the teleprompter. No public speaker has ever been so widely identified with the teleprompter as President Barack Obama. In March 2009, the news media had a field day with Mr. Obama's unprecedented use of a teleprompter at his second primetime presidential press conference. "What kind of politician brings a teleprompter to a news conference?" asked Associated Press reporter Ron Fournier.[2]

During the 2008 campaign, political commentator Dean Barnett observed that candidate Obama could "turn a phrase better and do more with a teleprompter than any other modern era politician." However, Barnett had also attended an Obama speech where the candidate had no teleprompter. Instead, he relied on 3x5 cards for his speech notes. Without the teleprompter, Barnett said, Obama's delivery "was halting and unsure. He looked down at his obviously copious notes every few seconds throughout the speech. Unlike the typical Obama oration where the words flow with unparalleled fluidity, he stumbled over his phrasing repeatedly."[3]

Reporters noted that President Obama brought the teleprompter into settings where it had never been used before, such as the East Room and the Grand Foyer of the White House. The teleprompter's glass panes made it hard for camera crews to get unblocked shots of the president's face. "It's just something presidents haven't done," said presidential historian Martha Joynt Kumar. "It stands in the middle between the audience and the president because his eye is on the teleprompter."[4]

President Obama's reliance on the teleprompter has produced some odd presidential moments. On St. Patrick's Day 2009, with the prime minister of Ireland at his side, President Obama bizarrely thanked himself—then realized he was reading the Irish prime minister's remarks.[5] On another occasion, he was introducing guests in the course of the speech, when he realized that he was repeating himself. He paused for several seconds, staring at the teleprompter while the audience waited uncomfortably, then he told the teleprompter operator, "Go ahead. Move it up. I had already introduced all you guys." The audience laughed nervously.[6]

Contrast these episodes with one of the most famous teleprompter mix-ups in history—President Bill Clinton's 1994 State of the Union speech. The moment President Clinton stepped onto the platform and looked at the teleprompter, he knew he was looking at the wrong speech. As the assembled guests applauded, he leaned over to Vice President Al Gore and told him about the mix-up. Gore left the stage.

As the applause died down, Clinton decided to simply make light of the problem. He thanked the audience for their applause, then said, "I'm not at all sure what speech is in the teleprompter tonight, but I hope we can talk about the state of the Union." The audience laughed—and President Clinton continued talking, ad libbing a tribute to former House Speaker Tip O'Neill, who had passed away two weeks earlier. As President Clinton continued his impromptu remarks, it took the technical crew nine agonizing minutes to load the correct speech into the teleprompter. When the speech text started rolling, Clinton seamlessly transitioned from his off-the-cuff remarks to his prepared text, and his performance that night drew high praise from the public and the press.

The greatest communicators of all are those who don't need a teleprompter, who don't need a script or a set of notes, but can face an audience and speak straight from the heart. They are the communicators who are always in control, who never panic, and who are never at a loss for words.

If you want real security and confidence as a speaker, then you've got to throw away the script, toss out the notes, and come out from behind the lectern. And the way to do that is to practice your signature speech until you reach a point where you feel that your notes are no longer helpful—they've become a hindrance. Notes tie you down. Lecterns nail your feet in one place.

The only real security you have as a speaker is right between your ears. When you have that speech locked down and tucked away in your memory, nothing can take it away. You don't have to worry about a missing page from your script, or about fumbling your index cards, or about a teleprompter with the wrong speech. Everything you need to dazzle an audience is right inside you.

Now you are ready for anything.

Breaking the Barriers

I have given thousands of speeches from 3x5 note cards. It took me a long time to let go of those cards. But giving up my note cards was the best thing I ever did as a speaker. Once I made that transition, I was no longer "delivering speeches." I was having conversations with my audiences. I was telling my stories and sharing my insights in a conversational way. Oh, my talks weren't always grammatically pristine, but a conversation isn't supposed to be.

In fact, that sense of impromptu conversation actually creates a sense of intimacy and trust between you and your audience. The audience senses that you are not just broadcasting material to a faceless crowd. You are connecting with every individual in your audience in a personal way. You aren't dispensing information. You are sharing from the heart, thoughtfully and spontaneously.

When I broke free of the lectern, I discovered a connection with the audience I have never known before. Because I have discovered this freedom, I know you can do it, too. After all, look at where I started! Remember that the man writing this book was once the tongue-tied student in Miss Bullard's speaking class. If that shy, insecure lad can grow up to do what I do now, imagine what *you* can accomplish!

I went through each of the stages of public speaking that I described to you earlier:
• Step One: No Confidence
• Step Two: Clutching the Security Blanket
• Step Three: Taking Baby Steps
• Step Four: Time to Solo
• Step Five: Total Freedom!

The only regret I have is that I took so long to transition from one stage to the next. My advice to you: Don't wait! Speed up the process! Transition faster!

Stop clinging to your notes. Stop clutching the lectern. Start breaking the barriers. Move closer to your audience. When you become totally free to move about and speak without notes, people will say to you, "How do you do that? How do you remember what you're going to say?"

The answer is simple: Practice, practice, practice. You deliver your speech hundreds and hundreds of times until you learn it, hone it, and can deliver it in your sleep. You accept every speaking opportunity and invitation. You speak at schools, churches, service clubs, and at every conceivable opportunity. In short, you pay your dues. Forget about getting paid at first—just get up and speak. Get the practice now, and the money will come later.

One of the greatest public speakers I've ever heard was the late UCLA basketball coach John Wooden. He was still making public appearances well into his 90s. On the stage would be a single chair, and Coach Wooden would come out with his cane and a microphone clipped to his lapel, and he'd sit down. Then, for the next hour, in his soft-spoken professorial manner, he would speak without notes, delivering a logically structured, easy-to-follow, life-changing talk. He'd share his pyramid of success, recite lines of poetry (some memorized from his youth, some written by himself), and tell fascinating stories from his early life and his coaching career. Many times, I sat there like a sponge as he spoke, absorbing every drop of wisdom that fell from his lips.

I'm glad I have Coach Wooden as a public speaking role model. I'm not in my 90s, but I was recently diagnosed with multiple myeloma, a cancer of the plasma cells in the bone marrow. This health issue makes it harder for me to stand for a long time. So, like Coach Wooden, I sometimes sit on the stage in my chair and talk to the audience, and I tell them I'm doing so in honor of Coach Wooden. I am only half-joking. I want to emulate him and his easygoing manner of having a conversation with his audience.

The secret to becoming a great public speaker is not learning to speak with grand oratorical flourishes, but learning to be yourself, learning to communicate naturally and confidently, and learning to simply connect with an audience. It all begins with being organized and prepared.

Next, we're going to look at the best way to open your speech.

3

The Grand Opening

Comstock

Fifteen seconds—that's all you've got. If you have not won over your audience in the first 15 seconds of your speech, you are in for a struggling hour. What do I base that on? My own personal experience as a speaker.

When I stand in front of an audience, I make eye contact, I read expressions and body language, which gives me a good sense of what people are thinking. Even before you get up to speak, people begin to evaluate you. They make judgments (largely unconscious judgments) about whether they trust you, whether they like you, whether they think you are going to impact their lives or bore them to tears.

You have a very narrow window of opportunity in which to make a good impression and gain your listeners' trust. In my experience, that window of opportunity lasts about 15 seconds. They're looking at you and asking, "If I give this person an hour of my time, will it be worth my while? Will this person give me action points I can implement right away—or kill an hour of my life? I could be reading the paper, clearing emails, texting, getting work done. I could even be on the golf course! Instead, I'm trapped in a meeting room with this clown for the next miserable hour!"

See what you're up against? So you'd better not be boring. And you'd better not waste your listeners' time. You've got to be entertaining, informative, charming, witty, and captivating—right from the first word. If your presentation is dull or pointless, if you seem insecure or unhappy to be there, then you'll be playing to a hostile crowd.

Everything about you—from the way you dress to the way you carry yourself, from the expressiveness of your face and eyes to the confidence of your stride and body language, from the tenor of your voice to the words you speak—must make an immediate positive impression. If you lose your listeners in those first critical 15 seconds, it will be very hard to get them back. I'm not saying it's *impossible* to get them back, but why dig yourself a hole right at the start?

People often ask me, "Why do you speak?"

I've chosen this career for many reasons, but I think the number-one reason is that *I love the challenge.* I think public speaking is one of the great challenges in life. I walk into a room with several hundred people who may have heard of me but don't know me. We are strangers to each other. Their attitude is generally along the lines of, "Okay, let's see what you can do. We want to check out your stuff." And in those first 15 seconds, you'll either lock them in or lose them.

Grand Openings

My first eye-opener about the importance of a grand opening came in the late 1970s when I was general manager of the Philadelphia 76ers. I had befriended Alvin Dark, the longtime National League shortstop and Major League Baseball manager. Alvin is a man of faith, and I invited him to speak at a Sunday night service at our church in

Cherry Hill, New Jersey. After I introduced Alvin to the congregation, the very first words out of his mouth were, "In 1974, I said, 'Charles Finley is going to hell.'"

Instantly, Alvin had that whole sanctuary riveted.

"Now," he continued, "that's not exactly what I said, but that's how it ended up in the newspaper. I was speaking at a church, and during the question-and-answer session, somebody asked about Charlie Finley's eternal destiny. And I said, 'If he doesn't accept Christ, he's going to hell.'"

Well, that was just the first 30 seconds of Alvin's talk—and I was sitting there with my hair standing up on my neck. I was thinking, "What an attention-getting launch to a talk! It's like a Sandy Koufax fastball, *whoosh!*"

Everyone in the auditorium paid close attention to everything Alvin said that night. And I learned an important lesson in how to launch a speech.

Up until that time, I had begun all my speeches with a soft, even weak opening: "It's so good to be here. Thanks for inviting me. It's great to be here with you all. How is everybody doing tonight?" Then I'd run off a monologue of jokes.

I thought that such an opening would help me connect with my audience, but I was wrong. That kind of opening is tentative. It lacks power; it lacks authority. In short, it's boring. From the day I heard Alvin Dark speak, I decided I would find a way to rivet my audience from the very first sentence, just as he did. Today, there are no preambles to my speeches; I get right to it.

When you think about it, all the great speakers of history have done exactly that. Take, for example, a famous speech delivered on the afternoon of Thursday, November 19, 1863. President Abraham Lincoln journeyed by train to the battlefield at Gettysburg, Pennsylvania. What were the first words out of his mouth? "How are you all doing? It's good to be here in Gettysburg. I'm glad so many of you could come out today. It's great to get away from Washington, and to come out here to Pennsylvania and see all the fall colors. And you know, it was around 87 years ago when our fathers brought forth this country."

By now, if you know any American history at all, you know that this is *not* how President Lincoln began the Gettysburg Address. When he stood to speak, the very first words out of his mouth were, "Four score and seven years ago, our fathers brought forth on this continent a new nation, conceived in liberty, and dedicated to the proposition that all men are created equal." He began by reminding his audience exactly why America had been founded in 1776. This young nation, only 87 years old, had been founded for the purpose of setting people free and guaranteeing their God-given right of equality. Though only two minutes in length, the Gettysburg Address is arguably the greatest speech in American history—and it was delivered without any preamble or preliminary remarks.

President Lincoln's speech wasn't the only speech delivered that day. The famed orator Edward Everett of Massachusetts was also on hand that day, and he gave a speech that lasted *two full hours*. Everett began his speech with the words, "Standing beneath this serene sky, overlooking these broad fields now reposing from the labors of the waning year, the mighty Alleghenies dimly towering before us, the graves of our brethren beneath our feet, it is with hesitation that I raise my poor voice to break the eloquent silence of God and Nature." And so it went for the next 119 minutes. Today, Everett's two-hour speech is forgotten, along with its lengthy and tiresome preamble—and Lincoln's two-minute speech is not only remembered, but memorized by schoolchildren across America.

Great speeches begin with a bang. Unfortunately, all too many speeches begin with a whimper. As a father of 19 children (four birth children, 14 by adoption, one by remarriage), I have been to a lot of high school and college commencement speeches. I'm sure you've been to your share of commencement speeches, too. They are usually, to put it charitably, dry as dust. But they don't have to be. Great commencement speeches always start with a bang.

When science fiction writer Ray Bradbury addressed the Caltech class of 2000, he began with these words: "This is fantastic! I never made it to college—I didn't have enough money—and I decided I was going to be a writer anyway. And the reason I was going to go to college was all those girls. So it's a good thing I didn't go."

Comedian Jon Stewart gave the commencement address at his alma mater, William & Mary, in 2004. He opened by saying, "Thank you! I had forgotten how crushingly dull these ceremonies are. Thank you! My best to the choir. I have to say, that song never grows old for me. Whenever I hear that song, it reminds me of nothing."

Feminist novelist Ursula K. Le Guin, author of *The Left Hand of Darkness*, opened her "Left-Handed Commencement Address" at Mills College in 1983 with these intriguing words:

"I want to thank the Mills College Class of '83 for offering me a rare chance to speak aloud in public in the language of women. I know there are men graduating, and I don't mean to exclude them, far from it. There is a Greek tragedy where the Greek says to the foreigner, 'If you don't understand Greek, please signify by nodding.' Anyhow, commencements are usually operated under the unspoken agreement that everybody graduating is either male or ought to be. That's why we are all wearing these 12th-century dresses that look so great on men and make women look either like a mushroom or a pregnant stork."

When Apple co-founder Steve Jobs gave the commencement address at Stanford in 2005, he began, "I am honored to be with you today at your commencement from one of the finest universities in the world. I never graduated from college. Truth be told, this is the closest I've ever gotten to a college graduation. Today, I want to tell you three stories from my life. That's it. No big deal. Just three stories."

Novelist Barbara Kingsolver, author of *The Poisonwood Bible*, began her 2008 commencement address at Duke University with this attention-getting statement: "The very least you can do in your life is to figure out what you hope for. The most you can do is live inside that hope, running down its hallways, touching the walls on both sides. Let me begin that way: with an invocation of your own best hopes, thrown like a handful of rice over this celebration. Congratulations, graduates."

And fright-meister Stephen King began his 2001 commencement address at Vassar College with this grabber: "I have to tell you the scary truth, because that's my job. You know the old proverb, don't you, about the woman who carries the drowning scorpion across the raging stream? Once they're on the other side, it stings her and as she staggers to her knees, dying, she reproaches it for ingratitude. 'C'mon lady,' it says, 'you knew I was a scorpion when you picked me up.' And you knew I was the scary guy when you picked me for this job, so deal with it."

These are all grand openings for great commencement speeches. Each is unique, each is an attention-getter, and each is a great way to make a powerful impression during those crucial first 15 seconds.

A Great Takeoff Means a Great Flight

I travel a great deal. I'm in and out of airports all the time. One thing I've learned is that there's nothing like a smooth, comfortable, well-coordinated flight. You get through security quickly, and you get out to the gate. The plane is on time. You nestle down in your seat, and soon the pilot starts taxiing out to the runway. You feel those powerful engines rev up as the plane hurtles down the runway. Soon, you feel that elevator-lift as the plane comes off the tarmac and soars into the air. It's so smooth that a glass of water on your tray wouldn't spill a drop.

Up you go, among the clouds—it's a beautiful feeling. You just know the rest of your flight is going to be a dandy. That's every traveler's dream. The key to a great airplane flight is a great takeoff. A nice, smooth takeoff means that you are probably going to have a comfortable flight.

The same is true of a great speech. If your speech gets off to a strong start, if you have your opening buffed and polished, rehearsed and perfected, and if you can deliver your opening smoothly and confidently, then odds are you're going to deliver an outstanding speech.

So my challenge to you is to have that opening nailed to perfection. The moment you get up to speak, you should know exactly what you're going to say, and the pace and cadence at which you will say it. You should have it measured out, practiced and timed, with all of your hand gestures, facial expressions, and vocal inflections well-rehearsed.

If you impress your audience with the first 15 seconds of your talk, they'll be on your side for the rest of your talk. Even if you make mistakes later on, even if the rest of your speech isn't as smooth and polished as the opening, your audience will be rooting for you. They'll be sympathetic to you. They'll give you good nonverbal feedback (nodding, smiling, applause), and they will hang in with you.

I've found that you can rarely go wrong by opening with a story. So, when I give my talk called "Finding the Will to Win," my first words out of the block are:

> "Several years ago, I had a speaking engagement in Fort Myers, Florida. After I finished, I was at the book table, signing books. The lady who helped me set up the book table was named Joy Millis. I'll never forget her. She was a chatty type, and she had some interesting experiences to talk about.
>
> "'Some years back,' she said, 'I was on a flight, reading a book, and I looked up and recognized one of my fellow passengers. It was Johnny Unitas, the great Colts quarterback. I couldn't believe I was sharing the same flight with him. After the plane landed, I went to him and said, 'Mr. Unitas, would you please sign this book for me? And please don't sign it 'Good luck' or 'Best wishes' like you would sign it for anyone else.'
>
> "'He said, "Well, ma'am, how would you like me to sign it?"
>
> "'I said, "Sign it with the best piece of advice you ever got from one of your coaches."
>
> "'So Johnny Unitas signed the book, "To Joy—Win!—Johnny Unitas."'"

And that story segues into my talk on how to be a winner.

I have also developed a talk I call "The Seven Sides of Leadership." I open that talk with this story:

> "I'm a civil war buff. Anytime I'm in a region of the country near a Civil War battle site, I make it a point to visit that site. I once had a speaking engagement in Norfolk, Virginia, and I wanted to visit Fort Monroe, an important port during the Civil War. The union launched some major battles from there. Abraham Lincoln visited there early in the war. Jefferson Davis was incarcerated in one of the cells at Fort Monroe, and you can still visit that cell today. It's a fascinating and moving piece of American history, and it also remains an active military base.

"As our tour guide showed us around the base, I saw a series of buildings off to the right, and I asked our guide, 'What goes on in there?'

"He said, 'Sir, we're doing a lot of teaching there. We are training young soldiers.'

"'What do you teach them?'

"'A number of topics—but primarily, we teach them leadership, sir.'

"That got my attention. I looked at the doorway of one of the buildings, and over the doorway was a simple two-word inscription: 'Leadership Excellence.' And I've been thinking a great deal about leadership excellence ever since."

And then I launch into the main points of my talk.

Your Thousandth Speech Should Sound Like Your First

When you get up to give your signature speech, the speech you've spent hours and hours preparing, the speech you've delivered a hundred times before, you have to convince your audience that you are delivering it for the very first time. Your goal is to make it seem that you have hand-crafted this message just for them. And even though it is your signature speech, you need to tailor it for each particular audience. If you are just "phoning it in," if you haven't taken the time to shape that message for that specific audience, then you're cheating your audience.

It's important to know exactly who your audience is, what they do, what they care about, and why they've chosen *you* as their speaker. And it's important, right at the beginning of your speech, that they hear you make a reference to their company or organization and that they know you're familiar with them and this is not just a cookie-cutter presentation to an anonymous collection of faces. Even if you have given that talk a thousand times, if you particularize your speech for that audience, if you make all the right references at the beginning of your speech, they will come away saying, "What a great speaker! That message was just for us!"

If your audience gets the impression that this was just another gig to you, that you don't truly care about them, then count on this: You are here today and gone tomorrow. They will not be impressed one bit. You won't be invited back. You won't get referrals. In fact, you'll probably damage your reputation as a public speaker.

Whatever you do, *don't* commit the public speaker's most embarrassing sin. I speak from experience, because I've done it. What is that sin? It's when you stand up in front of your Cleveland audience and shout, "Hello, Cincinnati!" It's when you show up at the Coca-Cola sales convention with a can of Pepsi in your hand. It's when you commit the unforgivable error of mistaking you audience's organization for their fiercest competitor.

In my case, it happened a few years ago when I was speaking at a small college in the mountains of North Carolina. In the course of my speech, I referred to the school by name—or so I thought. As it turned out, I had actually used the name of the rival school a few miles down the road! A grumpy-looking guy in the audience called out to me, interrupting my speech and correcting me in front of the whole audience. That was the lowest point of my speaking career—even worse than my very first speech in Miss Bullard's ninth grade class. It's almost impossible to recover from a gaffe like that.

NBC *Today* show host Ann Curry had a similar experience when she gave the commencement address at Wheaton College in Norton, Massachusetts. During her speech, she named some of the school's most illustrious alumni, including CBS *60 Minutes* correspondent Lesley Stahl, horror film director Wes Craven, evangelist Billy Graham, and United Airlines Flight 93 hero Todd Beamer. Unfortunately, the only person on Curry's list who actually went to that college was Leslie Stahl. All the others went to a *different* Wheaton College—the Christian liberal arts college in Wheaton, Illinois. After the event, a blushing Ann Curry wrote a letter to the Massachusetts Wheaton, saying, "I am mortified by my mistake."

Boy, can I empathize!

Imagine if our Orlando Magic organization brought in a motivational speaker to speak to our 250 employees at the beginning of the season, and suppose he began, "As a long-time fan, it's a thrill for me to be here, speaking to the Miami Heat!" That event would unravel so fast, his head would spin! And believe me, that's an easy mistake to make. When you do a lot of public speaking, it's easy to fall into the "Where am I today?" trap.

So you've got to study your audience and the organization you're speaking to. Make sure you refer to the organization accurately. If you mess that up, you're going to be looking for a hole to jump into. No matter what you say after that, no matter how scintillating and charming you may be, you'll never get the audience back on your side after that mistake.

Don't Be Nervous—Or, at Least, Don't Show It

Nervousness is part of public speaking. Always has been, always will be. And that's okay. A little bit of nervousness is good for your performance. It gives you energy that you can channel and put to good use.

Never apologize for being nervous. You might feel like a squadron of butterflies is dogfighting in your stomach, but your nervousness rarely shows to the audience. Put on a confident smile, carry on with your speech, and soon you'll feel genuinely confident.

President John F. Kennedy was afflicted with terrible stage fright—but the public never knew it. In his televised debates, public speeches, and press conferences, he always seemed cool, relaxed, and in total command of the situation. The one factor JFK could not control was his hands. Whenever he was in front of an audience, his hands shook uncontrollably. To keep his hands from betraying him, he kept them below the lectern. Occasionally, he'd bring up his right hand to make a point—but he'd quickly dropped it out of sight again, lest it give him away.

You may feel like everyone is thinking, "That poor speaker is a nervous wreck!" In reality, your listeners are admiring your calm, relaxed demeanor.

Before you speak, as you're waiting for the applause to die down, take a few deep calming breaths. Deep breathing floods your system with oxygen. It steadies your voice and helps you to think more clearly. If you feel yourself getting nervous and starting to take quick, shallow breaths, just pause thoughtfully, take a breath, then go on with your presentation.

It often helps, as you begin your talk, to find a few supportive faces in the crowd. Make eye contact with those people. Smile, and they'll smile back. The friendliness of their reception will help put you at ease. I refer to these dear friends as "facial cheerleaders." After the talk, I always seek them out to thank them for the key role they played in my presentation. They are usually unaware of how much their friendly smile means to me as a speaker, so I like to make sure they know I value their support.

Do you ever get a case of the jitters when you get up to speak? Don't worry about it. And don't let a little nervousness at the beginning throw you off-stride. You've practiced. You know your material. You're off to a good start, and you're going to be great!

What about mistakes? Hey, everybody makes a few. Nine times out of 10, if you don't tell people you made a mistake, they'll never catch on. If you get lost for a moment, don't call attention to it. Your audience can't see your outline, so how will they know if you are lost or not? Pause, take a deep breath, tell a story, keep moving forward, and no one will ever know the difference.

If you stumble or get tongue-tied, make a joke about it, and move on. Your audience will love the fact that you can kid yourself about your mistakes. If you handle the occasional flub with a sense of humor, you'll actually win your audience over. It tells your audience, "I'm not perfect. I'm just like you: a real human being."

Finally, author and speaker Bob Phillips offers a daring suggestion for launching your speech. "Use the power of silence," he told me. "After you are introduced, don't say a word. Look the audience over, eye to eye. Let the silence hang there until it becomes uncomfortable, almost unbearable. You want the audience to wonder if you've forgotten what you planned to say. A hush will come over the room. Then, when you finally break the silence, the first words out of your mouth *must be powerful.* That's how you nail them. It's fun to watch that sense of release ripple through an audience after you have kept them in suspense with the power of silence."

Or, as Mark Twain once said, "The right word may be effective, but no word was ever as effective as a rightly timed pause." I have used the power of silence many times to open my own speeches. It's an amazing experience—and I urge you to try it. You step out on the stage, you say nothing—and it really hushes the room. That expectant hush gives you the perfect dramatic moment in which to deliver your grand opening.

In the next chapter, we're going to talk about how to outline and structure your speech for maximum effectiveness and impact.

4

Know Where You're Going

Comstock

They called Ronald Reagan "The Gipper" because of his role in the 1940 motion picture *Knute Rockne, All American*. Reagan played Notre Dame quarterback-halfback George Gipp, who led the Fighting Irish in rushing and passing in 1918 through 1920. After Gipp's final game against Northwestern in November 1920, he came down with strep throat and pneumonia. Hospitalized, he grew weaker and weaker.

Coach Knute Rockne visited the Gipper on the night of December 13, just hours before the young football star died at age 25. For years afterward, Rockne refused to discuss his last conversation with George Gipp.

Time passed, and Rockne's Fighting Irish fell on hard times. In 1928, the worst season of Coach Rockne's career, he took his 4-2 Irish to Yankee Stadium for a game against undefeated Army. Rockne knew that, after the Army game, his embattled Irish faced almost certain losses to Carnegie Tech and USC. If the Irish didn't defeat the Cadets, they faced a 4-5 season—Rockne's first-ever losing season. He was determined to beat Army.

The game began and Notre Dame battled Army to a scoreless standstill in the first two quarters. In the locker room at halftime, Rockne saw that his players were spent. They had fought hard, but their will to win was fading. Rockne had an ace in the hole—a speech he'd been planning and saving for just this occasion.

"Well, boys," he said, looking at his team, "I'm going to tell you a story I've kept to myself for years." Instantly, every eye was locked on Coach Rockne.

"None of you ever knew George Gipp," he began. "The Gipper was long before your time. But you know what a tradition he is at Notre Dame. The last thing he said to me was, 'Rock, sometime, when the team is up against it, and the breaks are beating the boys, tell them to go out there with all they've got and win just one for the Gipper. I don't know where I'll be then, Rock, but I'll know about it, and I'll be happy.'"

There was a long silence, then Rockne concluded, "That's what he said. And this is the day. And you are the team."

Coach Rockne let those words sink in—then his team leapt to their feet as if on command. They rushed out of the locker room, almost knocking the doors off their hinges.

The game resumed—but early in the third quarter, disaster befell Notre Dame. A 41-yard Army pass set up a touchdown—and a 6-0 Army lead.

The determined Notre Dame team refused to accept defeat. They marched down the field until they reached Army's one-yard line on fourth-and-goal. As halfback Jack Chevigny fought his way into the end zone, he shouted, "That's one for the Gipper!"

Later, Notre Dame tight end Johnny O'Brien caught a long pass at the Army 10-yard line, shook off a pair of tacklers, and dashed across the goal line for a second touchdown. From the sidelines, O'Brien's teammates shouted, "Another one for the Gipper!"

Army fought back and managed to get the ball to Notre Dame's one-foot line on fourth-and-goal. Army tried to punch the ball through—but the Irish defensive front held. Army failed. Game over.

Inspired by the story George Gipp and the halftime speech of Coach Rockne, the Fighting Irish beat Army and went on to a winning record of 5-4. Notre Dame's 1928 season may have been less than stellar, but Coach Rockne's halftime speech became legendary. That speech, which Coach Rockne had planned and saved for years, spelled the difference between victory and defeat—just when it mattered most.

What is the speech that defines your life, your career? Will you know what to say when you're up against it, when the breaks are beating you, and you need that one speech that will turn defeat into victory? Great speeches don't just happen, they don't just come off the top of your head. Great speeches are the result of thoughtful, deliberate crafting and structuring.

In the next few pages we'll look at the structure and outline of your speech. We'll discover how to craft a game-changer of a speech—the kind of speech that will define you as a speaker and transform your career.

How to Measure Your Influence and Impact

I am a connoisseur of speeches. I have sat in the audience for literally thousands of speeches. As a consumer of the spoken word, I know what I like. I think I have a pretty good idea of what most people are looking for in a speech.

Audiences don't just want information. They can get information by reading a book or searching a website. Audiences want a *life-changing experience*. They come to a speech hoping that the speaker will have some insight, some plan to offer, some wisdom from on high that will create a "Eureka!" moment. It might be an insight into how to become a more winning coach, a more effective salesperson, a more successful leader, a more savvy investor, or a more popular author.

The listeners in your audience want to come away with three or more points that they can put into action immediately, as soon as they walk out of the auditorium. They want the speaker's ideas and advice to be so clearly and logically organized that they can take good notes. They want the stories the speaker tells to be pegged to each principle, not just tossed haphazardly throughout the speech.

When I speak, I always invite the audience to take notes. When you encourage note-taking, you'd better give people material that is "noteworthy" and easy for them to follow. So whenever I speak, I like to give the audience numbered points, then continually reinforce those numbers so the audience knows exactly where they are in the outline of the speech.

As I go deeper into my talk, there's an increasing possibility that I might lose some of my listeners. So, I'll pause every now and then and say, "Let's review where we are. The first side of leadership is vision, the second side of leadership is communicating your vision, the third side is people skills, and now let's go to the fourth side ... ."

If your speech is well-organized, you always know where you are, and so does your audience. Many experts will tell you that one of the first rules of speaking is: "Tell them what you're going to say, then say it, then tell them what you said." That's a good rule. In a well-organized speech, you're constantly giving quick reviews so that your audience is always oriented. You tell them where you're going, you tell them where you are, and you tell them where you've been. This way, they can review their notes, they can see the entire flow of your message, and they can fill in any gaps where they might have missed a point along the way.

If you have crafted a clear, well-organized speech, you'll discover that something wonderful happens at the end of every speech. People will come up to you and say, "Look at this! I took pages of notes! Would you please sign them for me?"

This happens to me all the time. It's a great feeling when somebody shows you the notes they took on your talk. Sometimes, that person will say, "I missed one point. What was point number four?" And you can plug that in for them. They know exactly what they missed, because every point was numbered.

When people show you their notes and ask you to autograph them, it says that they were able to follow you, they were excited about what you had to say, your content impacted them at a deep level, and they will come back and review these notes again and again. This is how you measure your influence on your audience.

A Simple, All-Purpose Outline

Now, let's look at a basic outline for your speech. This format is simple to use, and it will work with almost any subject, in any setting, with any audience. By using this format, you will always be able to give a clear, well-organized speech that your audience will be able to follow and understand with ease.

Following is the basic outline:
- Opening story
  ✓ Rivet the listeners' attention with a story that introduces your topic.
- Transition to the body of your speech
  ✓ Tell them what you're going to say. Introduce the actions you want them to take.

- Story and point 1
- Story and point 2
- Story and point 3
- [Stories and additional points as needed]
- Conclusion and closing story
    - ✓ Tell them what you said (recap the main points).
    - ✓ Drive home the actions you want your listeners to take.
    - ✓ Memorable big finish!

There's your simple, all-purpose outline. Whether you're a coach talking to your team or the Boosters Club, or a CEO speaking to your board or an investors meeting, or a politician speaking to voters, or a military officer firing up your troops, this is a great outline for any speech. It's endlessly adaptable to different subjects. It's easy to follow. It forces you, the speaker, to think about the needs of your audience and to include strategically placed stories that will illustrate principles and rivet the listeners' attention. It's hard to go wrong with a speech that follows this outline.

Your speech should be about one specific topic. It should be well focused on that topic, and anything that's extraneous—anything that distracts from that topic—should be eliminated. Then break down that one topic into sub-points. You should have at least three sub-points.

Swen Nater is a retired professional basketball player who played for Coach John Wooden's legendary UCLA Bruins before going on to a long career with teams in the ABA, NBA, and European leagues. For years, I've urged Swen to compose a speech about the values and leadership lessons he learned as a player for Coach Wooden. "Swen," I said, "none of Coach Wooden's players knew him better than you did. You played for him, you spent countless hours with him, and nobody could speak more authentically about him. You have a unique message to share that audiences would pay to hear."

Finally, Swen said, "Pat, I'm going to do it. I'm going to compose that speech." I was honored when Swen asked me to coach him as a public speaker. He worked hard and came up with a 10-point outline he calls "The Ten Keys to Leadership." So we went over his outline together, and I suggested some ideas for organizing his talk for maximum impact. I hope to see Swen deliver that talk to an audience soon.

I've also encouraged another friend, Michael Mink, to get on the speaking circuit. Michael is a Los Angeles–based writer who has written for *Investor's Business Daily* for the past two decades. He's amassed an archive of more than 500 columns about successful people in all fields. "Michael," I said, "you may have the most interesting talk anyone could ever give. You've studied and interviewed some of the most successful people in history. You could comb through your columns and identify the common traits of all those successful people. That would be an amazing speech!"

Well, he's done it. When I heard him deliver that speech, I said, "Now, that's a talk that will grab everybody's attention. You've nailed it!" He had two or three great stories to illustrate each trait—and there wasn't a dull moment in that talk.

Both Swen and Michael built their talks on the same basic outline I've laid out in this chapter. It works for them. It will work for you.

No matter how accomplished you are as a public speaker, there's always room for improvement. I'm constantly striving to be better tomorrow than I was today. I think the worst sin of public speaking is the sin of complacency, the sin of thinking, "I'm good enough. I don't want to hear what I do wrong as a public speaker. I just want to be as good as I am now."

I hear this attitude a lot in the public speaking world. I've met many professional speakers who do not want any counsel, advice, input, or coaching. They don't want to be trained. They don't want to improve. They think, "I'm getting paid well, and my name carries me. Audiences like me just the way I am."

Yet many of these same speakers could achieve so much more for themselves, for their careers, and for their audiences if they would be willing to learn a better way to organize their talks. Their presentations would be more memorable and practical; their reputations would rise. And who knows? They just might find themselves in greater demand, earning much higher speaking fees.

What About PowerPoint?

People often ask me, "What about PowerPoint® or other visual aids? Do you use them?" Well, I don't. I'm "old school," and I rely on speaking alone to communicate my message. I'm not opposed to PowerPoint, but I think it can become a crutch. I've seen it used badly. And when PowerPoint is used badly, it becomes a distraction, not an aid.

I also believe that any speaker who plans to use PowerPoint should also be prepared to go on with the show. After all, what if the computer or projector fails? A speech that relies totally on PowerPoint, and which can't be delivered without it, invites the wrath of Murphy's Law.

Audiences often get caught up with the pictures and words on the screen, and miss the most important points you're making as a speaker. That's why I've made a point of holding an audience for an hour with nothing but my presence, my message, my voice, and my gestures. I'd rather paint word pictures for people then flash a picture on a screen. I'd rather tell stories that come alive in people's imagination than put up cute videos for them to watch. Yes, it's a challenge, but it's tremendously satisfying when you pull it off well.

I know that some people have to use PowerPoint when they speak. It's a requirement of their job. Also, PowerPoint can be an excellent way to convey facts, figures, and charts that don't communicate well verbally. The key is to use PowerPoint thoughtfully and with an awareness of its limitations. Following are some tips for making the most effective use of PowerPoint:

- *Keep it simple.* Select one basic, legible serif typeface (such as Times Roman) for easy-to-read body text (e.g., bullet points) or a sans-serif typeface (such as Helvetica or Arial) for emphasizing headings, and use that typeface throughout. Avoid large blocks of type in ALL CAPS, which can be difficult to read. Use a comfortably large, upper- and lowercase font. Avoid layouts that are "busy" and crowded and overly ornamented. Avoid flashing, annoying images and animations. A design that is simple and consistent throughout is easy to read and understand.

- *Keep it brief.* Don't force your audience to read long paragraphs of type. Use PowerPoint only for bullet points, phrases, brief quotes, and for emphasizing key concepts and takeaways (concepts you want your listeners to take away from your speech).

- *Use pleasing colors and images.* Avoid garish, lurid, clashing colors that will give your audience a headache. Make sure that the type contrasts well with the background for easy reading (for example, never make audiences strain to read black type against a red background).

- *Use blank slides to avoid distracting your audience.* After you make your point with PowerPoint, click to a blank slide—a slide that is either solid black or a solid background color with no type or image. This will make your listeners focus on you as you talk, and will keep them from being distracted by the previous slide.

- *Make sure your PowerPoint slides are appropriate for your audience.* The same visual presentation that works for a roomful of kids would be embarrassing to show in a roomful of business executives. Know your audience. Don't speak down to them or insult their intelligence through your slides and images. Make sure your visual presentation works seamlessly with your spoken word to enhance your total presentation.

- *Practice.* Make sure you have rehearsed your PowerPoint presentation numerous times so that you can focus on your speech, not on the mechanics of your slide show. A problem-plagued visual presentation can kill a great speech.

- *Don't let PowerPoint ruin your delivery.* The rules of great speech-making still apply whether you are using PowerPoint or not. You have to communicate directly with your audience—don't look down at your notes, or at the PowerPoint controls, or at the screen behind you. Have a conversation with your audience. Maintain good eye contact. Remember, the audience came to hear you speak, not to look at pictures or words on a screen. Make sure the focus is on you and your message, not on the screen behind you. If the PowerPoint comes between you and your audience, you are better off without PowerPoint.

You don't need gadgets and props to be an effective speaker. Your challenge is not how to liven up your talk with bells and whistles, but how to be a more effective, persuasive communicator. The key to your effectiveness is within you and the way you organize your message, not in your PowerPoint slides.

"Tear down this wall!"

In mid-1987, President Ronald Reagan was preparing to go to Berlin and give a landmark speech before the Brandenburg Gate. White House speechwriter Peter Robinson had recently returned from West Berlin, where he had talked to ordinary Germans, asking them what they thought of the Berlin Wall. He wrote a strong, stirring speech—and the centerpiece of that speech was a demand, issued to Soviet president Mikhail Gorbachev, to "Tear down this wall."

President Reagan read the speech during a weekend at Camp David, then he met with Robinson and other top advisors on Monday. Reagan opened the meeting saying that he loved the speech, especially "that passage about tearing down the wall. That's what I want to say to them, that the wall must come down."

That very line, however, sent shockwaves through the corridors of the State Department and the National Security Council. Even Howard Baker, Reagan's chief of staff, tried to talk his boss out of saying, "Tear down this wall." For almost a month, arguments raged between the Reagan White House and the diplomatic corps. The diplomats warned that such blunt language would offend the Soviets. But the Gipper stood his ground.

Shortly before President Reagan was to leave for Germany, he met with his deputy chief of staff, Ken Duberstein, for a final review of the speech. Duberstein suggested that there was still time to edit out the "Tear down this wall" line. Reagan said, "Ken, I'm the president, aren't I?"

Duberstein replied, "Yes, Mr. President, we're clear on that."

"The line stays in."

So Reagan went to Berlin. On the very morning that he was to deliver the speech, June 12, 1987, the State Department was still cabling alternate versions of the speech, hoping to change Reagan's mind. But Ronald Reagan went to the Brandenburg Gate, stood before the vast crowd, and said, "General Secretary Gorbachev, if you seek peace, if you seek prosperity for the Soviet Union and Eastern Europe, if you seek liberalization: Come here to this gate! Mr. Gorbachev, open this gate! Mr. Gorbachev, tear down this wall!"[1]

Two years after President Reagan's Brandenburg speech, the German people tore down the wall. A short time later, the Soviet Union collapsed.

What is the message you want to deliver to the world? What is the speech you are determined to deliver, regardless of opposition from friends and foes alike? What is your "Tear down this wall" moment?

Craft your message. Organize it for clarity and maximum impact. Tell your audience what you are going to say, then say it, then tell them what you said. Give them action steps. One of the hallmarks of a great speech is that your listeners can put your principles and insights into practice *immediately*. You are not just spouting platitudes and theories; you are planting your message in people's minds, and you are changing their lives. Make an impact on your audience, and change your world.

In the next chapter, we're going to take a closer look at how you can connect with your audience through the strategic use of stories and humor.

5

"Let Me Tell You a Story…"

Stockbyte

Actress-comedienne Bonnie Hunt has appeared in dozens of films and was the host of the syndicated TV talk show *The Bonnie Hunt Show* for two years. Early in her career, she was late and bedraggled for an audition for a film role. Her agent, who knew she delighted in making up funny tall tales, begged her not to make jokes at the audition.

When Hunt sat down with the producers, they asked why she was late. "Well," she said, "it's like this: While I was driving to the studio, a brick hit my car and broke the window. I stopped to check the damage—and somebody stole my purse out of the car. That's why I look like this—all my makeup was in my purse! And just when I thought things couldn't get any worse, I opened my car door, and this truck came out of nowhere and ripped the door right off my car! I could've been killed!"

After the audition, Bonnie was certain she had blown any chance of getting the part. But her agent called her and said, "The producers loved you! They said that ridiculous story you told was what sold them. I know I begged you not to tell any of those crazy stories, but I guess you knew best."

"What crazy story?" Hunt said. "Everything I said was 100-percent true!"

And it was.

Your Witty, Charming Self

We have come to the two key aspects of your speech that determine the difference between good and great, the difference between a speech that is interesting and a speech that has impact. I'm talking about *stories* and *humor*. These two elements can make or break your speech.

First, let's look at humor. This is a controversial issue among experts on public speaking. Some counsel against using humor—especially joke humor. It's true, most people are not naturally good joke-tellers (and most people are not nearly as funny as they think they are). Telling jokes—story-form humor with punch lines—is an artform that requires a sense of rhythm and timing that most people don't have. It's easy for a joke to fall flat—and there's nothing more embarrassing than that awkward, embarrassed silence after a fizzled punch line.

But I'm convinced that simple, natural, engaging humor can be mastered. And over the years, I discovered again and again that *audiences love to laugh*! Laughter is the universal language. Studies have shown that laughter can help cure cancer. So there's no doubt in my mind that laughter can liven up a speech and help you connect with your audience. So I encourage you to work hard at polishing up your natural sense of humor. As speaking legend Zig Ziglar once told me, "Make your audience laugh within 30 seconds of getting up to speak. It opens their minds, and they become more teachable."

I'll admit it; I'm not a naturally funny guy. I'm not a standup comic by any means. But I've spent my career mastering sharp one-line humor and wry observations that always seem to click. Years ago, when I was a young sports executive, I was deeply impacted by speakers I heard in the sports world. I saw how they could captivate an audience with humor, and how laughter created a bond between the speaker and the audience.

Pete Carlesimo was the first full-time director of the National Invitation Tournament and the father of NBA coach P.J. Carlesimo. A longtime college sports figure in the New York City area, Pete did a lot of public speaking—and I never missed a chance to hear Pete speak. I was fascinated with his ability to make audiences laugh.

In college, Pete was a Fordham football teammate of Vince Lombardi, and often joked about how little classroom work he had to do as a football player. "Don't tell me I never saw a classroom," he'd say. "I've seen plenty of classrooms. They were those rooms with desks and blackboards in them. I know, because we used to pass by some classrooms on our way to football practice, and sometimes we'd look inside."

Carlesimo was in demand as a speaker at Fordham awards dinners and fundraisers, primarily because he made audiences laugh. His delivery was deadpan—but he always had the room in stitches. He once opened a talk by saying, "When my secretary told me I had been selected to speak at this event tonight, I was very surprised. I don't have a secretary."

One of Pete Carlesimo's biggest fans was Johnny Carson, who frequently booked him as a guest on *The Tonight Show* on NBC. Pete loved appearing on Carson's show. Though he was usually booked for a six-minute segment, Johnny would keep him on through a couple of commercial breaks, 20 minutes or more.

Another speaker who had a great early influence on me was my friend Bob Vetrone, Sr., the veteran Philadelphia sports writer. Bob grew up in South Philly, and I once heard him tell how he became a college basketball fan in December 1937. His uncle took him to Convention Hall to see Stanford play Temple. The game was a sellout, and Bob and his uncle were among the thousands of fans turned away at the gate.

"I didn't even get to see the game," Bob recalled, "but I was an instant basketball fan. Here were all these people standing in the snow, trying to get into a basketball game. I figured right then and there, this has *got* to be one heck of a sport!"

Bob Vetrone could get an audience laughing one moment, then dabbing at their eyes the next. I once heard him speak movingly of his friendship with former Villanova coach Al Severance. Bob and Al roomed together in Lexington, Kentucky, when Bob went to broadcast the 1985 NCAA championship game.

"I got up on the morning of the big game," Bob said. "Al was still sleeping, and I didn't want to disturb him. So I went downstairs to make some phone calls and get some breakfast in the coffee shop. When I got back to the room, Al was on the floor of the bathroom. He'd been shaving when he just collapsed and died. Al was one of my first really close friends. He coached Villanova for 25 seasons, and he was Villanova's biggest fan. What a shame he didn't live to see that game. My emotions were up and down all day—and when the Villanova Wildcats beat the Hoyas 66 to 64, it made me cry. I couldn't stop thinking, 'Al, you missed a great game.'"

Another great influence on my early speaking career was Frank Layden, the longtime NBA and college coach. I heard Frank speak on a number of occasions, and he would absolutely captivate a room with his sparkling sense of humor. He once talked about trying to coach a young man who was talented but unmotivated. Frank recalled, "I said, 'Son, what's your problem? Is it ignorance or apathy?' The young man shrugged and said, 'Coach, I don't know, and I don't care.'"

Frank was a golfer, but a grouchy one. "I hate golf," he once told an audience. "There are no referees. There are no coaches. There are no teammates. There's nobody to blame when you mess up; you can't even blame your wife. For some reason, though, we all keep playing the game. I play it, too, but I hate it."

Early in my speaking career, I used humor as an icebreaker at the beginning of the speech. But with experience, I've found that it works better to weave an occasional "laugh line" into the main body of my talks. Just don't overdo it. You're not a standup comic, and neither am I, so use just enough humor to surprise and delight your audience. Too many one-liners and your audience may get the impression you are not serious enough for your subject matter. Don't try to be Leno or Letterman; just be yourself, your naturally witty and charming self. As sportscaster Dick Enberg once told me, "I love to hear an audience laugh. Humor is your best ally. You can win your audience early if you can get them smiling and laughing. They will relax, and so will you."

I was fortunate, during my years in Philly, to build a friendship with a schoolteacher from Lancaster, Pennsylvania, Ken Hussar. For 35 years, Ken and I have been collecting one-line humor, all clean and guaranteed to work from the podium. With Ken's help, I collected the best material in *The Ultimate Handbook of Jokes for Coaches, Leaders, and Speakers* (available from Coaches Choice in 2012). The material is categorized by topic, so it's easy to find just the right one-liner for any speech, any audience. If you're looking for a good humor resource for your speeches, I suggest you give it a try.

Where Does Humor Come From?

Humor is serious business. Author, speaker, and retired basketball player Jay Carty told me, "Humor is the anesthesia that allows the scalpel to go deep. Humor is not an icebreaker to me. It takes me deeper into the topic." Those are wise words. When you inject humor into your speech, you're not just trying to entertain, not just going for a cheap laugh. You should use humor strategically and thoughtfully, with a clear purpose of taking your audience more deeply into the serious subject matter of your speech.

People often ask me, "Where can I find humor for my speeches? Where does funny material come from?"

Much of it comes from observing life. You simply take time to observe and comment on the little details of everyday situations—details that most of us are simply too busy to notice. We laugh at these observations because we recognize those situations. They strike a responsive chord. We say to ourselves, "Yep, that's exactly what happens to me!"

A master of observational humor is Florida's own Dave Barry. In one of his syndicated columns, he talked about his decision to paint his lawn. "I don't mean my whole lawn," he explained. "I just mean this one circular spot that suddenly, mysteriously turned brown, as though it had been visited by a small UFO or a large dog."

Barry went on to explain how he recruited his six-year-old son, Tyson, to help him with the painting project. They got Tyson's watercolor set and some brushes, then went out to the brown spot on the lawn. "We were working on a blade-by-blade basis," Barry recalled, "and after a while we got tired of dark green, so at Tyson's suggestion we switched over to purple, then red, then orange, and when we were done we had converted what had been a dull and unattractive area of the lawn into an area that looked as though somebody had just thrown up several pounds of semi-digested jelly beans."[1]

Dave Barry makes us laugh by starting with a situation familiar to every homeowner—an annoying brown spot in the lawn. As he relates his story, the details get stranger and more and more absurd. It's hard to know where Barry's original observation ends and his imaginative hyperbole begins. But he starts by observing the little details of life that most people pass by without noticing.

I suggest you keep a notebook or computer file of stories and incidents and observations. Write them down as soon as they happen to you. Make a point of noticing everything that happens whenever you spend time with your kids, or take the dog for a walk, or visit relatives, or interact with co-workers and friends. You never know when your everyday life might serve up a funny anecdote for your next speech.

Also, be observant when you read. You'll find humorous stories for speeches in books and magazines, practically everywhere you turn. When you find a good story, save it. Clip it, write it down, or type it into your computer. It doesn't matter if the story is usable right now are not. If it seems like a good story, save it. And someday, when you're writing a speech and need a funny anecdote, you'll remember that story, and you'll have it ready for use.

When you use humor, make sure you never attack the audience. Don Rickles could get away with ridiculing audience members. You almost certainly won't. If you want a safe target for "insult humor," pick on yourself. Self-deprecating humor is often a good way to get the audience on your side. It shows that you're a good sport, that you can take a joke, and that you don't take yourself too seriously. If you have to tell a joke at someone's expense, let the joke be on you.

I learned this lesson the hard way some years ago at a speaking event in Phoenix. I got to the dinner early, checked with the meeting planners, and asked who in the audience would be good targets for some one-line humor. I asked who plays golf, who roots for a certain college team, and then I said, is there a really heavy guy here who can take a joke about his weight? I got the names of these individuals, and at the start of my speech, I plowed into my Johnny Carson routine, got great laughs, and thought I had scored big time. I finished my talk, went back to my hotel room, and prepared to fly out on a red-eye back to Orlando that night. Then the phone rang. And I thought, who could that be? Well, I soon found out. A man with a quivering voice said, "My name is _____. I was the target tonight in your opening concerning my weight." He said, "I just want you to know this is the worst night of my life. I was humiliated, I was mocked, and totally embarrassed. Why did you pick on me like that?" Wow, what do you say? I said, "Sir, I am so sorry. I got your name from the meeting planners, who said it would not be a problem. I did that little routine all in fun, nothing personal at all, but obviously I stepped over the line and wounded you. All I can do is apologize profusely and ask for your forgiveness, and I promise I will never do that again in the future." I flew home to Orlando that night with a heavy heart. I will never make that mistake again.

One final thought on humor: Always keep it clean. You may be tempted from time to time to work an off-color story into your speech. You might think, "These guys won't mind if I work blue." Don't count on it. Dirty humor almost always backfires. There are always a few people in the audience who will take offense. You may get a few laughs, but it's not worth the risk. Always keep it clean.

The two best ways to make an emotional connection with your audience are laughter and tears. If you can move your audience to laughter or tears, you have hit a home run. These two emotions are more closely linked than you might realize. If you can get your audience to laugh, you'll be amazed at how in mere moments you can tell a heart-tugging story and bring that same audience to tears.

Become a Storyteller

In May 2010, Amazon.com CEO Jeff Bezos gave the commencement address to the graduating class at Princeton. He opened with a story from his boyhood. "As a kid," he said, "I spent my summers with my grandparents on their ranch in Texas. I helped fix windmills, vaccinate cattle, and do other chores."

His grandparents belonged to a Caravan Club—a group of people who traveled around the country, living in an Airstream trailer. "I loved and worshipped my grandparents," Bezos recalled, "and I really looked forward to these trips."

On one trip, when Jeff was about 10 years old, his grandparents were in the front seat and he rode in the back. He enjoyed using his math skills to do calculations, such as working out their average grocery expenses or gas mileage. Jeff's grandmother was a heavy smoker, and Jeff hated the smell of her cigarettes. He had heard an anti-smoking advertisement on the radio, which said that every puff of a cigarette takes a certain number of minutes off a person's life. So young Jeff Bezos did the math in his head, then he poked his head over the front seat, and tapped his grandmother on the shoulder.

"Grandma," he said, "at two minutes per puff, you've taken nine years off your life!"

Jeff expected to be applauded for his clever use of his math skills. But that's not what happened. Instead, his grandmother burst into tears.

At this, Jeff's grandfather pulled the car over to the shoulder of the highway. He got out of the car, opened Jeff's door, and led him back alongside the Airstream. Jeff wondered if he was about to be scolded or forced to apologize.

"My grandfather looked at me," Jeff Bezos told the Princeton grads, "and after a bit of silence, he gently and calmly said, 'Jeff, one day you'll understand that it's harder to be kind than clever.' What I want to talk to you about today is the difference between gifts and choices. Cleverness is a gift; kindness is a choice."

What a great story! And what a great introduction to his theme. Jeff Bezos told the story of a young boy who was very clever at math—but who needed to learn that kindness is more important than cleverness, and that in order to be the kind of person he ought to be, he needed to *choose kindness*, and not simply rely on his cleverness.

It's a story that makes the point memorable. I'm sure that, now that you have read that story, you'll remember it for years to come. Moreover, when you do, you'll remember exactly what the point was: It's more important to be a person of kindness than to be a person of cleverness.

That's the power of stories. It's the power to illuminate a message. It's the power to make a message unforgettable. It's the power to make *you* unforgettable as a speaker. Stories are the most powerful tools in a speaker's toolkit. Forget your PowerPoint presentations, your animated graphics, your movie clips, your bells and whistles. Instead, focus on telling a great story. We are hardwired to retain stories, not PowerPoints. If you want to be a great public speaker, become a great storyteller.

Bestselling author and motivational speaker Ken Blanchard once told me, "Be a great storyteller. Every concept you share in your speech needs to be backed up by a story. Great speakers are observers of life, and they relate their observations through stories."

Stories always stick in the mind. We are hungry for stories. We can never get enough of them. I have read countless stories to my children at bedtime. I would no sooner finish reading one story, and my kids want another. And another. And another. Children will eventually fall asleep—but only after eight or nine stories.

One of the best examples of the power of stories is the *Chicken Soup for the Soul* book series. In the early 1990s, two successful motivational speakers, Mark Victor Hansen and Jack Canfield, collected a hundred and one of their favorite stories. They took their manuscript to dozens of publishers, but every publisher turned them down. Finally, Health Communications, Inc., of Deerfield Beach, Florida, decided to take a chance on the *Chicken Soup* concept.

Well, the *Chicken Soup* phenomenon exploded. The first book was followed by sequels, *Chicken Soup for the Mother's Soul*, *Chicken Soup for the Preteen Soul*, *Chicken Soup for the Grandparent's Soul*, *Chicken Soup for the Soul: Teens Talk Relationships*, and on and on. More than 100 million copies have sold worldwide—and there is no end in sight. The book that was rejected by almost every publisher in the industry became the publishing phenomenon of the past two decades. Why? Because people can't get enough of stories.

Stories have a strategic place in your speech. Each story must be anchored to a point or principle, not just tossed in at random. Stories do more than merely perk up the audience's interest. They reinforce your message. They instruct. They underscore. They make an emotional connection with your listeners.

Never read a story. Tell it. Better yet, act it out and bring it to life! Spellbind your audience. Practice your storytelling so you can tell stories with energy, movement, gestures, and facial expressions. When you tell a dramatic story from your own experience, try lowering the volume of your voice. You'll see your audience lean in and listen more intently. It makes your stories more intimate and gives them greater impact.

Leadership guru Patrick Lencioni once shared this advice with me: "When speaking, let the audience into your life. Make them insiders, and they'll root for you. They'll feel they are part of your team." Colin Powell agrees. He once said, "You have to let your listeners into your world. You use personal stories to do that."

There's nothing wrong with telling stories about other people, stories you picked up from books or from the Internet. But whenever you can personalize a story and connect yourself with that story in some way, you give those stories more impact.

For example, I have written two books about legendary UCLA basketball coach John Wooden. The most recent was *Coach Wooden: The Seven Principles That Shaped His Life and Will Change Yours*. I was just completing work on the final chapter in the book when I received a call informing me that Coach Wooden had passed away at the age of 99. I was saddened, not only because I had lost a dear friend and mentor, but because I had hoped to present a copy of that book to him on his 100th birthday.

In that book, I tell a number of stories from Coach Wooden's life. Some are stories that Coach Wooden himself shared with me, while others are stories that I found in the books Coach Wooden has written or which were written about him. From reading about Coach Wooden, I learned that, after his wife Nell passed away on March 21, 1985, he began a tradition of writing a love letter to her on the 21st day of every month. In those letters, he told Nell how much he loved and missed her, and how he looked forward to seeing her again. After writing each letter, he would place it in an envelope and set it on the pillow on Nell's side of the bed.

When I told that story in my book, I could have simply related it as a story I had found in a book by another author. But I was able to personalize that story, because on one of my visits to Coach Wooden's apartment, he took me into his bedroom and showed me that little bundle of love letters, tied with a yellow ribbon, sitting on Nell's pillow. I could even describe the lump in my throat when I thought about how much this man loved and missed his wife.

When you personalize a story, you give it added depth and dimension. Even a minimal amount of personalizing can make a big difference. For example, you could preface a story by saying, "I'll never forget where I was when I heard about the space shuttle Challenger," or "I'll never forget what I was doing when I heard that our Navy SEALs had gotten bin Laden." You don't have to be an eyewitness to those events. Just recalling your emotions when you heard the news will stir the emotions of your audience.

Everybody loves a good story. Whenever I see an audience starting to drift away, when I see their eyes start to glaze over and their attention falter, I know exactly what to say: "Now, let me tell you a story ... " Instantly, all my listeners are sitting up in their chairs, leaning forward, totally engaged.

My friend and speaking coach Alfonso Castaneira (whom you'll meet in Chapter 9) explained it to me this way: "Memorable speakers know how to take an audience on an emotional journey. Storytelling is the most powerful way to take your audience on an emotional rollercoaster ride. We respond to emotional forces of love, fear, hurt, anger, and sorrow. To reach the humanity of your audience, you *must* reach their emotions. If you touch an audience at a deep emotional level, they will remember you, they will be persuaded, they will follow your leadership to the ends of the earth, and they will be motivated to *act*."

The Power of Storytelling

Some of the best advice I received came from Janet Thoma, one of my editors at Thomas Nelson Publishers. In the late 1990s, when I was working with her on my books *Go For the Magic* and *The Magic of Teamwork*, Janet told me, "Save your stories. Write them down as soon as they happen to you, because if you don't, you'll forget them. File them by categories. Then when it's time to write a speech or a book, you'll have your stories all written down and ready to use."

That piece of advice, from one of the best editors I ever worked with, changed my life. I began saving and cataloging all of my stories from my own life, my family, my career, and the many famous people I came in contact with. I saved stories I found in books and magazines. I saved stories people told me. The moment I read or hear a great story, I tuck it away—and I have all of those stories at my fingertips the moment I need them.

I go to church every Sunday. I've noticed that whenever I leave the church service and walk to my car, I may not remember much of what our pastor said in his sermon that day, but I will never forget his stories—and the points those stories made. The stories stick with me for days and even years after the rest of the sermon is forgotten.

Most of the great leaders of history were storytellers. Certainly, Jesus of Nazareth was a storyteller—though his stories are known as parables. As you read through the life of Jesus in the New Testament, you see that he does most of his teaching and preaching through stories. In fact, the Gospel of Matthew tells us: "Jesus spoke all these things to the crowd in parables; he did not say anything to them without using a parable."[2]

Abraham Lincoln loved to listen to stories—and he loved to tell them. He regularly used stories to make a point. Historian Doris Kearns Goodwin credits President Lincoln's father, Thomas Lincoln, with instilling a love of stories in young Abe. Thomas Lincoln was "possessed a quick wit, a talent for mimicry, and an uncanny memory for exceptional stories. These qualities would prove his greatest bequest to his son."[3]

Goodwin reveals that Abraham Lincoln's love of storytelling began quite early in his life: "He would climb onto a tree stump or log that served as an impromptu stage and mesmerize his own circle of young listeners…. This great storytelling talent and oratorical skill would eventually constitute his stock-in-trade throughout both his legal and political careers. The passion for rendering experience into powerful language remained with Lincoln throughout his life."[4]

Lincoln's skills as a storyteller were essential to his roles as lawyer, leader, public speaker, and president. "No one could equal his never-ending stream of stories," wrote Goodwin, "nor his ability to reproduce them with such contagious mirth…. But Lincoln's stories provided more than mere amusement. Drawn from his own experiences and the curiosities reported by others, they frequently provided maxims and proverbs that usefully connected to the lives of his listeners. Lincoln possessed an extraordinary ability to convey practical wisdom in the form of humorous tales his listeners could remember and repeat."[5]

Ronald Reagan was another president who loved good stories, and used them often in his public speaking. When the late president's son, Michael Reagan, was a guest on my radio show, he told me about his father's gift for storytelling:

"William Clark was one of my father's closest friends and advisers throughout his career. And Judge Clark once explained something to me about my father that I had never realized before. 'Michael,' he said, 'your father was not just a storyteller. He spoke in parables. Even his jokes were parables. Whenever he wanted to teach people something, he would teach it in the form of a story.'

"What an insight! I had lived with my father all those years, and I had never seen that before. Dad's stories were always entertaining—but if you really listened to him, if you really thought about what he was saying, you could always find a deeper truth that you can apply to your life. During the Cold War, he liked to tell jokes about life in the Soviet Union. Here's one of his favorites:

"In the Soviet Union, there was a 10-year wait to buy an automobile. Only one out of seven families in the Soviet Union owned cars. Those families had to go through a long process and a lot of paperwork, and they had to put up the money in advance. So one Soviet citizen saved up his money and went to the government showroom and plunked down his cash. And the official in charge said, 'Okay, comrade, in 10 years you can come back and get your car.' The citizen said, 'Morning or afternoon?' And the government official said, 'Ten years from now, what difference does it make?' And the citizen said, 'The plumber's coming in the morning.'

"Now, that's a funny story! But it has a serious point to it. My father was giving his listeners an insight into what life was like in the Soviet Union. Stories like this one showed that life under communism is hard, and people have to put up with shortages and long waits and a lot of bureaucratic red tape. He was telling you, 'People want to be free, but there's no freedom under the Soviet system.' But he was telling you in a subtle way, without hitting you over the head with it. If you wanted to just laugh at his joke, that's fine. But if you wanted to think about the meaning of his parable, my father always gave you plenty to think about."

All the great speakers of history were storytellers. Stories don't just entertain. They instruct. They make us think. They make us remember. We remember stories long after the rest of the speech is forgotten. That is the power of storytelling.

Humor and stories make a human connection between ourselves and our audiences. We all love to laugh, and we all love a good story. Whenever you speak, you can never go wrong if you say, "Let me tell you a story…"

In the next chapter, we are going to learn how to bring your speech to a grand conclusion.

6

"In Conclusion…"

Comstock Images

The great American author Mark Twain once attended a fund-raising dinner for a charitable cause. The after-dinner speaker got up and began extolling the virtues of the worthy charity. As the speaker seemed to draw his oration to a conclusion, Twain was favorably impressed and thought that the charity was worthy of his support. He decided to donate $100.

But the speaker continued to speak. On and on he droned. Twain became annoyed with the speaker's pompous and excessive verbiage. Drumming his fingers on the table, Twain wondered why the man didn't simply shut up. Twain decided to cut his contribution in half.

Still, the speaker talked. And talked. Twain closed his eyes, pretending to sleep. The speaker droned on. Twain decided to cut his contribution to $10.

The speaker continued speechifying with no end in sight.

Finally, after the third repetition of, "In conclusion … ," the speaker finished his remarks and sat down. The ushers passed the collection basket around the tables. When the basket reached Mark Twain, his charitable mood was gone. Instead of making a contribution, he withdrew a dollar from the basket and passed it along.

Many speakers are guilty of overstaying their welcome, of "talking past the close of the sale." Great speakers know that less is often more, and that there is a limit to the human attention span—and the endurance of the human tailbone.

Every speech needs a crisp, strong conclusion. Whenever you get up to speak, your speech should be focused on that conclusion. You should build toward that conclusion, and once you've delivered that conclusion, you're finished. Bam! Done! Applause, applause!

In Chapter 3, I compared a speech to an airplane flight. A great takeoff means you're probably in for a good flight. But every great takeoff needs a great landing. A great takeoff won't do you much good if, on reaching your destination, you roll right off the end of the runway. You have to begin with a polished opening and conclude with a polished ending, delivered with power and enthusiasm, sounding as if you are saying it for the very first time. You must practice that conclusion, nail it, and own it, in order to deliver it with power, punch, and audience-pleasing finality. That's the equivalent of a silky smooth, feather-light landing on the tarmac.

The ultimate tribute to any speech is a standing ovation—and the key to a standing O is an ending that knocks 'em dead. Later in this chapter, I'm going to show you how *I make sure* I get a standing O every time I speak!

End With a Bang!

You can rock your listeners back on their heels with a stunning opening, get them laughing uncontrollably with your witty one-liners, bring them to tears with your powerful stories, and have them eating out of your hand for a whole hour—then blow it all away with a weak, insipid ending. If your big finish becomes a big fizzle, you might as well not have come.

There is one ending that I hear from professional speakers again and again, and it is the worst ending of all: "Well, thank you all for coming. It was great to be with you. I appreciate this invitation. Yadda, yadda, yadda … ." That's a speech that doesn't actually come to an end. It just dribbles away, like a faucet with a leaky washer.

Can you imagine Abraham Lincoln concluding his Gettysburg Address with these words: "… that this nation, under God, shall have a new birth of freedom—and that government of the people, by the people, for the people, shall not perish from the earth. Well, thanks once again for coming out today. And could we have a round of applause for Governor Andrew Curtin for making this event possible? Yes, and another hand for Edward Everett, who spoke earlier. Ed, take another bow. Well, you've been a great audience, get home safely, and may the Lord bless you all." Now, that would *not* have gone down in the annals of great American speeches.

When a speech just trails off, the audience doesn't know when the speech is actually over. People don't know if it's time to clap or stand up and file out or head for the refreshment table or what. A speech that lacks a clear-cut *bang* of a finish leaves everyone in the room feeling awkward and uncertain. That's the last thing you want to do at the conclusion of your speech.

Your closing should leave as good an impression as your opening. Begin with a bang, keep a strong rhythm going through the body of your speech, punctuate that rhythm with attention-grabbing stories and brilliant insights, and then finish with a bang! From your first word to your last, make an impact on the emotions of your audience. There is no place in your speech where it's okay to slack off or let your audience down. You must keep your edge from beginning to end.

"Stay up! Stay up!"

In 1986, I left the Philadelphia 76ers organization and came to central Florida to help build a new NBA franchise, the Orlando Magic, from the ground up. One of the first and most enthusiastic supporters of this effort was Jacob Stuart, then-executive vice president of the Orlando Regional Chamber of Commerce. A physically imposing man with a dynamic personality to match, Jacob opened many doors for me. We could never have built this organization without him.

Orlando was one of six cities in the running for an NBA expansion franchise. In September 1986, I led the Orlando delegation to the NBA owners' confab in Phoenix. I was accompanied by Jacob Stuart, key investors Jimmy and Bobby Hewitt, and accountant Stewart Crane. I had the responsibility for making a 30-minute oral presentation to the NBA owners, explaining why Orlando deserved to get a coveted franchise.

I felt as if the future of central Florida was on my shoulders, and I was intensely focused on delivering the speech of a lifetime to those owners. Thousands of jobs, worldwide publicity, and literally billions of dollars were riding on that 30-minute presentation. Jacob and the others would be with me for moral support, but I would do all the talking. I was more nervous than I had ever been in my life, and I didn't sleep well the night before that meeting.

Finally the moment of truth came, and our delegation was ushered into the presence of the NBA owners. We handed out three-ring binders containing financial projections, marketing plan, architectural renderings of the proposed arena, press clippings about our promotional efforts, and more. The binders were printed with the slogan "Orlando Believes in Magic!"

I knew it was up to me to persuade the owners. Charts and graphs and architectural drawings were fine, but every city in the running would have numbers and projections as good as ours or better. So as I launched into my pitch, I gave it everything I had, every erg of energy and enthusiasm I possessed. I used the same basic speech outline I laid out in Chapter 4. I punctuated my talk with stories about the people in our community, and the fact that all of central Florida was in a wild-eyed frenzy over the Orlando Magic and NBA basketball. I told them about a fan base so fanatical that the community had already purchased 14,046 season ticket reservations for a team that had no franchise, no arena, and no players!

When I reached the conclusion of that speech, I nailed it, bang! I felt good. I was wrung out like an old dishrag, but I had delivered the best speech of my career. I could tell from the faces of the owners that they were impressed. (Later, one of the owners, my friend Norm Sonju of the Dallas Mavericks, told me that he and the other owners were bowled over by the fact that I did an entire 30-minute presentation without notes.)

After the presentation, Jacob, the other delegates, and I headed for a nearby hall for a question-and-answer session with the media. Before I walked into the media room, Jacob got in my face and grabbed me by the shoulders. With his nose practically touching mine, he said, "Don't let down, Pat! Stay up! Stay up!"

Jacob is a perceptive fellow. I think he saw that I had given everything I had in that speech to the NBA owners—and now I was out of steam. I was so relieved to have the owners meeting over with that I was about to slack off as I stepped into the press conference. It was just as important to impress the media as it was to impress the owners! So Jacob pumped some of his abundant personal energy into my tired, sleep-deprived brain. The moment I heard him say, "Stay up! Stay up!" something within me sprang to life. I was revitalized and reenergized.

A new spring was in my step as I strode out onto the platform to face the reporters. I had the old energy in my posture, my eyes, and my voice. Every time a reporter fired a question at me, I heard Jacob's words in my mind: "Stay up! Stay up!"

It's important, whenever you speak, to keep your energy high right to the conclusion. That was the message of Jacob Stuart to me that day, and that's my message to you right now. Because Jacob wouldn't allow me to let down, Orlando got the thumbs up from the NBA—and there's been Magic in the air ever since!

If you're ever tempted to let your speech just trail off and peter out, remember this story. Remember the Orlando Magic. Remember Jacob Stewart's words to me that day: "Stay up! Stay up!"

A Standing Ovation Every Time

I promised to share with you my secret to getting a standing ovation every time I speak. Here's the secret: I cheat.

One of my most requested speeches is on leadership excellence. I talk about "The Seven Signs of Leadership," and I always finish with the seventh sign: servanthood—the importance of being a leader with a serving heart. I close on this note:

"I call my friend Swen Nater 'the Poet Laureate of America.' Swen has taken my Seven Signs of Leadership and condensed them into a few lines of poetry. So let me recap in verse form the seven leadership principles we've been talking about tonight:

> Seven things one must do
> to be a leader, right and true:
> A *vision* that is strong and clear;
> *Communicate* so they will hear.
> Have *people skills* based in love,
> And *character* that's far above.
> The *competence* to solve and teach,
> And *boldness* that has fearless reach,
> A *serving heart* that stands close by,
> To help, assist, and edify.

"In closing, let me tell you a story about Vince Lombardi. Back in the 1960s, Coach Lombardi led those legendary Green Bay Packers teams to NFL championships and Super Bowl triumphs. Every Thursday morning, before the start of practice, he would deliver a motivational talk to his team. That talk lasted about eight minutes. To this day, Coach Lombardi's former players can remember and recite those talks. They were powerful, energizing, and they would bring the hair up on the back of their necks.

"One of Coach Lombardi's players has said that those talks stirred up such strong emotions that the players couldn't stay seated while they listened. They would jump up and pump their fists, and they couldn't wait to get out on the practice field."

At that point, I pause and looked around at the audience. "Can you imagine it? Can you picture yourself in that locker room? Can you see Coach Lombardi striding up and down in front of you, thundering at you—

"'Winning is not a sometime thing! It's an *all*-the-time thing! You don't win once in a while. You don't do things right once in a while. You do them right *all* of the time! Winning is a habit. Unfortunately, so is losing.

"'There's no room for second place. There's only one place in my game, and that's *first* place. I have finished second twice in my time at Green Bay, and I don't ever want to finish second again! There's a second-place bowl game, but it's a game for losers, played by losers. It is and always has been an American tradition to be *first* in anything we do, and to *win*, and to *win*, and to *win*!

"'I firmly believe that any man's finest hour is that moment when he has worked his heart out in a good cause and lies exhausted on the field of battle—

"'Victorious!'"

And for those few moments, I have *become* Vince Lombardi. I can see the audience fidgeting in their seats. They can picture it. They can hear it. They can see it. Most of all, they can feel it—the energy of Coach Lombardi's passion for winning, transmitted through me to them. I go on to say, "You feel it, don't you? Coach Lombardi's players felt that same emotion—and they felt it so intensely that they simply couldn't remain in their seats. They had to get up on their feet!"

At that point, there is an electricity in the room, but it's *static* electricity. Nobody moves. Nobody wants to be the first to stand up, even though I have planted the emotion in all of them. So I'll walk out to the audience—and now I can *really* feel the electricity! "You feel it too, don't you? So how realistic do you want this to be? Coach Lombardi, through the power of his leadership, got his players motivated, energized, and *up on their feet.*"

And as I say that, I reach out to someone in the audience, and I take that person by the arm, and I gently lift that person up out of the chair. And that's all it takes. The crowd quickly follows. In seconds, they are *all* on their feet. What a moment that is! I continue: "When Coach Lombardi had motivated his players, when he had gotten them up on their feet, he issued them this challenge: 'Who's going to lead today?'

That's the last thing he said to them as they picked up their helmets and rushed off to the practice field. 'Who's going to lead today?' Ladies and gentlemen, that's the same question I leave with you: 'Who's going to lead today? More importantly, who's going to lead tomorrow? Will it be you? Or you? Or you?" Then I pause and say, "Go *get* 'em!"

And *boom*, it's over! Applause. Applause. Applause.

Now, did you notice how I got them on their feet before giving them that applause line? Is that a sneaky way to get a standing O, or what?

The ultimate tribute to any public speaker is a standing ovation. Whether you are a newcomer or you've been in this business for half a century, you never tire of the thrill that comes when you have hit the bull's-eye with a standing ovation. In order to get a standing ovation, you *must* end on an emotional note. Without emotion, you'll get polite applause, nothing more. Whether it's a personal story, or a story you got from a magazine or book, tell that story so that it pushes an emotional button. That's how you reach deep inside your audience and touch their souls and get them on their feet. That is how you have influence and impact on audience.

Next, we'll look at the all-important issue of how to prepare yourself, mind and body, for the challenge of public speaking.

7

Before You Speak—and After

Stockbyte

During the worst days of World War II, British Prime Minister Winston Churchill was the living embodiment of the unconquerable British people. His stirring, defiant speeches, broadcast by radio to the people of his nation, stiffened the iron will of England during its life-and-death struggle against Hitler and the Nazis.

On June 4, 1940, Churchill stood before the House of Commons and delivered one of his most famous speeches entitled "We Shall Fight." He said, in part, "We shall not flag or fail. We shall go on to the end. We shall fight in France, we shall fight on the seas and oceans, we shall fight with growing confidence and growing strength in the air, we shall defend our Island, whatever the cost may be. We shall fight on the beaches, we shall fight on the landing grounds, we shall fight in the fields and in the streets, we shall fight in the hills; we shall never surrender."

Churchill speeches have become so famous, so iconic, that most people assume that he was a naturally gifted speaker. Not so. In fact, he lacked confidence in his own speaking ability because he was painfully aware of some of his speaking impediments, including a slight lisp. In order to master the art of public speaking, Churchill devoted himself to hours and hours of preparation.

On one occasion, shortly before Churchill was scheduled to deliver an important speech, one of his friends found him pacing in his office, muttering to himself. When the friend asked Churchill why he was talking to himself, the old statesman winked and replied, "I'm just preparing a few impromptu remarks." (Churchill apparently believed in the old speaker's adage: "Rehearse everything—especially your ad libs.")

Winston Churchill believed in preparation for public speaking. He once said, "It takes an hour of preparation for every minute I speak."

How about you? Are you serious about public speaking—serious enough to put in an hour of preparation for every minute you speak? In speaking, preparation is all-important.

In this chapter, we will look at what you need to do *before* you speak in order to be ready and well-prepared. And, we'll also look at a few important things you need to do *after* you speak.

Weeks Before You Speak: The Pre-Call

Weeks before your speaking event, you should have a conversation with the planners or hosts of the event. I call this pre-event conversation the "pre-call." It's one of the most important things you do to have a successful speech. In order to shape your speech for your audience, you need to know everything you can about your audience: Who are they? Where do they come from? How can I best meet their needs?

Obviously, you will probably be using your signature speech, but you need to tailor and edit your speech just for that group. If they think that you're just recycling an old talk that you've given a thousand times before, they'll feel cheated—and it will damage your rapport with your audience.

It's easy to make mistakes, commit a serious faux pas, and get into trouble with your audience if you don't know who you are speaking to. You might deliver the same basic speech to a group of senior citizens and to a group of teenagers, but even though the essential content and structure of those two speeches might be the same, they had better sound like two *very* different speeches. And if you give a speech to a couple dozen guys at a men's breakfast group on Monday, you'd better not give the same speech at a Tuesday dinner event for 500 businesswomen. You need to tailor your signature speech for every individual event, every individual audience.

That's why the pre-call is so important. You can't tailor your speech unless you know your audience. Over time, I have worked out a series of questions that I always ask the event coordinator. These questions enable me to zero in on my audience:

- *How many people will be at the event?*
- *Where do they come from geographically?*
- *What is the gender breakdown?*
- *What is the age range?*
- *What is the professional or occupational background of the group?* I want to know if I am speaking to healthcare professionals, athletic coaches, retailers, corporate executives, or military professionals, so I can shape my speech to their exact needs and preferences.
- *Are they all from one company or organization, or do they come from many different organizations?*
- *How should I refer to them?* For example, should I refer to them as "the Chick-fil-A family" or the "General Electric team"? Is there a special "insider" designation I should use? How do they like to be known collectively?
- *How much time will I have with the group?*
- *As I prepare, what's the most important theme or topic I can bring to make a difference in their lives?* My signature speeches are on leadership, teamwork, quality, and personal motivation, and I need to know if I can tailor one of those talks for this group.
- *What is the theme of your meeting?* If the group has a theme or slogan for the event, I like to incorporate that into my talks.
- *What is going well for the people in your organization? Where are they struggling?* If possible, I like to address real issues that people are facing in their organization.
- *What is the dress code? Casual, business casual, business, or formal attire?* I recommend that you dress one notch above your audience. For example, if the dress code for the event is business casual, I would probably wear a jacket and tie. Fortunately, most of my audiences are dressed casually, so my usual speaking uniform is a Hawaiian shirt. My reason for wearing a Hawaiian shirt is simple: Have you ever seen anyone in a Hawaiian shirt having a bad day?

Whatever you wear, make sure it's pressed and looks good. You'd be amazed at how closely audiences examine the wardrobe of the speaker. At one speaking engagement in Cincinnati, I got into the elevator to go down to dinner, and a man and his wife also got in the elevator with me. The man looked down, then asked me, "How do you get such a shine on those shoes? It's hard to get really good leather shoes anymore." I thought, "Wow! It's amazing what people notice!"

A public speaker is a role model. People watch everything you do. They notice your haircut. They notice your fingernails. They notice how closely you shaved. No detail is unimportant.

- *Here's my cell number. What's yours?* When I get into town, I'll give the event planner a call to fine-tune the plan for the event. So it's crucial to have that person's cell number.

On the days leading up to and during the event, the event planner will not be in her office. She'll be running in 80 directions at once. So keep her cell number handy, and make sure you report in when you arrive. Put her mind at ease about one all-important detail: the speaker. When you call your event planner and say, "I just wanted to let you know I'm at the hotel and ready to go," that is sweet music to her frazzled ears.

When my questions have been answered, I recap our conversation to make sure I haven't misunderstood any of the information the event planner has given me: There will be this many people, they'll be coming from here and there, it will be X percent men and X percent women, most of them in such-and-such age bracket, I'll refer to them in this way, I've got so many minutes of speaking time, and my talk will be on such-and-such theme.

Event planners and audiences always appreciate it when you take the time to study them and personalize your message for them. The event planner also appreciates it if you take care of these details well in advance of the event. During the last few days before the event, and especially on the day of the event itself, that planner is going in a hundred different directions at once, dealing with emergencies, putting out fires. Make sure you don't increase the planner's stress load at crunch time. Get those questions answered well in advance. When game day arrives, you can let the event planner know you have everything under control.

The Evening Before You Speak: The Reception

Often, when you are about to speak at an event, there is a reception or dinner the night before. You are usually invited to meet and dine with the brass of the organization. They want to chat with you and get to know you. Now, you may have just arrived from the airport, feeling too tired to think straight, and in no mood for socializing. I know the feeling, but this is no time to slack off. You'd better grab a quick shower, freshen up, and get your game face on. Then go to the reception and be the life of the party.

I know, I know. You'd rather eat alone, read a newspaper, take a nap, or work at your computer. But if you give the impression that you are aloof and distant, then your talk the next morning is going to die. If people think that you are arrogant or temperamental, it will hurt you.

There have been times when I arrived the day before the event and attended the dinner party the night before. I was tired from the flight, I didn't know anyone, I didn't feel particularly chatty, so I slunk off to a corner and avoided conversation. Believe me, everybody knows who the speaker is, and they are watching him. If they see that you are not a joiner, if it seems that you are not happy to be there, that impression will impact how you are perceived and received the following day.

So I learned that, whether you feel like it or not, go around and introduce yourself. Put on a big smile, turn on the charm, and make some new friends. The next day, when you get up to speak, you won't be a stranger to the audience. You'll have people on your side who like you, who are ready to laugh at your witty asides. They'll feel like they know you, and they will be engaged with everything you say. Instead of judging you, they'll be rooting for you. That personal contact the night before can literally make or break your speech.

The Night Before You Speak: Early to Bed, Early to Rise

Another key piece of advice: No alcohol. I've known some speakers who like to sit in the bar the night before the big event, swapping stories and guzzling suds. I guarantee, it will take the edge off your performance the next morning. It will also ruin your reputation with many people in the organization. Sure, some people like that good ol' boy behavior, but you can count on it that many, if not most, will think less of you and see you as someone who lacks self-control and good judgment. It will undermine your image and your message. Ultimately, it will undermine your speaking career.

So stay away from the bar. Instead, plan on hitting the sack early and getting a good night's sleep.

Before you go to bed, lay out all your clothes for the following day. You don't want to be frantically searching for clean socks or your lucky tie while you are running late. Instead, make sure you have every detail worked out in advance so that your day goes like clockwork.

Set your alarm to get up early. Allow time to grab a newspaper or turn on the TV and catch the morning news. Check out *USA Today*, Fox News, and CNN. Why is that important? Because you never know when there might be a big event that grabs everyone's attention—and which you can weave into your talk. Make your speech as current and up-to-the-moment as it can be. The addition of current events to your talk will make your presentation more relevant, timely, and applicable. Your audience will notice and appreciate it.

The Morning of Your Speech: Physical and Mental Preparation

One reason I like to get up early is to have enough time for a good workout. I love to take a jog or make use of the hotel's weight room—get on the bike or the elliptical, or maybe jack a few weights. Exercise tunes up your body and gets your blood circulating, and that means more oxygen to the brain and better mental clarity throughout the day.

Whatever you do, don't skip breakfast. Allow time for a light but nourishing meal. Often, the event planners will have breakfast laid out for the attendees and speakers. Good nourishment also contributes to mental clarity and the ability to think on your feet. If you skip breakfast, you'll feel it right in the middle of your talk.

Avoid dairy products before you speak—they clog up your pipes. Fresh fruit, a bowl of oatmeal, scrambled eggs, toast and jam are all good fuel for a public speaker. But skip the yogurt or that glass of milk.

At least an hour before you speak, you should check out the room, familiarize yourself with the sound system, stand at the lectern, try out the microphone, sit in a few audience seats, and picture how you will come across to different parts of the room. If you wear a lapel microphone, and you must clip it to your left lapel, remember that turning your head to the right will cause your volume to diminish. I recommend that you do a sound test early, wear the microphone low and toward the middle of your body. Instead of turning your head from side to side, you may find that it works best to turn your entire body so that your voice is always projected directly into the microphone.

At some point in the morning, you should take time to prepare your voice. Your voice box is your most important anatomical instrument. You use it to project your ideas, your convictions, your passion, and your personality for the hour that you're on stage. So it's important to take a few moments to limber up your larynx.

If you are from my generation, you remember singer Andy Williams, whose signature song was "Moon River." In his autobiography, *Moon River and Me*, Williams wrote about his warm-up routine before every show, starting with a warm shower:

> When I'm in the shower—everyone sings in the shower, don't they?—I'll do some high notes and low notes, just to make sure they're all there, and I'll do some moos like a cow, because that really gets the vocal chords warmed up. The vocal cords are muscles, so they need that sort of preparation, like an athlete stretching before a race... .

I don't have any superstitions—odd socks, lucky mascots, or any of those kinds of things—but I do have one ritual. The last thing I do before I go on stage is check my fly. There are few things more embarrassing than realizing halfway through your act that your fly is open. By the time I've done all this, I'm raring to go out there and perform.[1]

The shower is an excellent place to do your vocal warm-ups. It's private, and the steam is good for your throat. You probably don't want any witnesses when you're doing your warm-up exercises. I've used Andy's trick of going "Mooo! Mooo!" like a cow. In fact, I've even tried crooning like Andy Williams, segueing from "Mooo!" to "Moooon River!" Like I said, it's best to have no witnesses.

After you warm up your voice, it's important to warm up the muscles in your face. I've had a number of speech coaches over the years, and one of them taught me a drill called "The Pumpkin-Raisin Drill." It's designed to get your facial muscles loosened up. You began with your mouth wide open, your eyes popped wide open, and your tongue sticking out as far as it will go. That's the pumpkin. You literally try to make your face look like a jack-o'-lantern. Then you instantly switch to a raisin, scrunching your face as small as you can make it. You wrinkle your nose, squint your eyes, and screw your mouth up tight. Do seven repetitions: Pumpkin! Raisin! Pumpkin! Raisin!

After seven reps, your face will feel like it has been through a wringer—but it will feel good! Now your face will be limber and expressive, capable of conveying all the passion and enthusiasm you feel inside.

This may sound silly to you, but you should never neglect your warm-up—especially your vocal warm-up. The last thing you want is to get up in front of an audience with a frog in your throat. That is every speaker's nightmare. Your throat is clogged, you can't seem to clear it, and your audience shifts uncomfortably, wincing at the sound of that croaking from your larynx. Meanwhile, people are offering you water and throat lozenges, and your speech is off to a horrible start. Don't let that happen to you. Do your warm-ups.

In 2005, *USA Today* reporter Cathy Lynn Grossman visited the North Carolina home of evangelist Billy Graham. She found Graham, who was then 86 years old and preparing for the 417th (and final) crusade of his career. He was exercising his vocal muscles, just as he had been doing for more than five decades of ministry. He was preparing for his final crusade as if it were his first. He never took his voice for granted. Instead, Graham explained that he practiced "like an opera singer does the scales." Then he demonstrated: "Yes. Yes. Yes. No. No. No."[2]

If you'd like to have a five-decade speaking career like Billy Graham, then follow his example. Do your warm-ups. Keep your vocal instrument limber. Use simple one-syllable words like *yes, no,* or *moo,* and take your voice up and down the scale. Practice deep notes and high notes. Give your voice a daily workout. Don't force your voice.

Don't abuse it; just exercise it, like you would any set of muscles. Take good care of your voice, and it will take good care of you.

Remember that the first 15 seconds of your speech are crucial. Your audience is sizing you up and forming that all-important first impression. Imagine the impression you'll make if the first words out of your mouth sound gargly and gross! Remember, you've got to get up on that stage and start wowing them from the very first syllable.

My daughter Karyn, who is a professional singer-songwriter in Nashville, introduced me to a wonderful product called Organic Throat Coat®, an herbal tea made from licorice root, wild cherry bark, slippery elm bark, and other ingredients that coat and soothe your throat, eliminating that froggy sensation. I recommend that, in the last 10 minutes or so before you go on stage, you sip a cup of *mildly* hot Throat Coat tea (be careful not to burn yourself). You can buy Organic Throat Coat in most drug stores and grocery stores.

Another suggestion: Just before you go on stage, tuck a sugar-free Ricola® throat lozenge in your mouth, between the gum and cheek, where it won't get in the way of your speaking. One lozenge lasts about 45 minutes, which should get you through most of your talk. If you have a 90-minute or two-hour talk, keep an extra lozenge in your pocket. Those soothing herbal vapors will keep your throat clear and give you confidence when you speak.

During the final 15 minutes or so before you speak, take time to meet and greet people as they come into the room. Mingle with the audience, make friends, make note of the few names, and establish rapport even before you speak.

Finally, in the last 30 seconds before you get up to speak, pause to focus your mind, clear away the chatter and distractions, meditate or pray, and center yourself. Breathe steadily and deeply as you focus your thoughts. As you breathe, you're pushing air through your vocal instrument, preparing it to project your thoughts, your stories, your vision to the audience. And as you breathe, you are drawing oxygen into your lungs, into your bloodstream, and sending it to your brain.

Think positive thoughts. Visualize your audience as a roomful of friends. Former Major League Baseball player and TV broadcaster Joe Garagiola once told me, "Whenever you get up to speak, act as if you're among friends and you're there for a nice little visit. Do that, and I guarantee you'll have a good time."

Those 30 seconds before you speak are very important. Use them wisely. Use them to prepare your mind, your heart, and your soul to give all you have to your audience. Then stand up, face your listeners, and speak the words you were born to speak.

Immediately Before Your Speech: Your Introduction

Most of us give very little thought to how we are introduced to the audience—until we sit and listen to our introduction! The person introducing you may have pulled up an old bio from 20 years ago, or a bio of another person with the same name as you, or a bio that is simply filled with embarrassingly wrong information. One of the worst things that can happen to a speaker is a long, boring introduction that puts your audience to sleep even before you say a word. It puts you at such a disadvantage that you may have to fight to regain your audience's attention for the rest of the talk.

Your introduction is truly one of the most crucial parts of your speech. Make sure that your introduction is concise and pithy, and that it tees up your speech instead of dragging it down. That means you should write your own introduction, keeping it concise and lively. Don't leave this all-important detail up to anyone else. If you want it done right, you must do it yourself.

After Your Speech: Let Them Know You

After your speech is over, you're not done. You still have work to do. Let your audience get to know you. Go out among the people, chat with them, shake hands, thank them for coming, and above all, show them that you genuinely care about them and you are glad to be with them. For me, this is always one of the most enjoyable aspects of public speaking—getting to meet the audience members on an individual basis. It's a chance to connect, to get feedback, to hear how my message affects real human lives. Getting to mingle with the audience is always a thrill for me.

When you have shaken the last hand and said goodbye to the last straggling audience member, you may think your work is finally done. Wrong. After you get home, take the time to write a letter or card of thanks. Not an email—a hand-written note. Mail it to your host or event planner, preferably with a modest gift. I usually send a signed copy of one of my books or an Orlando Magic gym bag or gift package. If it's a particularly big event, I sometimes send a gift card for a restaurant. People are deeply touched when the speaker does something extra for them.

Thank your hosts for everything they did to make your job easier and your stay pleasant. This is a very important step. It ties a nice ribbon on the entire event—and people will reward your kindness with more bookings in the future. This is how you build a connection and a relationship that will continue over the years.

Also, if you obtained that booking through a speakers bureau or agency, it's a nice touch to send a thank-you note and gift to your agent. They do a lot of work to make your life easier as a speaker. (We'll talk more about speakers bureaus in Chapter 8.)

Beware of "Brain Exhaustion"

The moment the applause begins and you take your final bows, there is a temptation to say, "It's over! Finally, I can let down!" You've been keyed up and focused on your presentation for days on end. Your mind has been a whirl of anxious emotions, but you got through it. Your brain is exhausted, and finally you can relax, right? Wrong! Don't let "brain exhaustion" ruin the finish of a great speech, as it ruined the speech of the New Jersey road commissioner more than a century ago. The following notice[3] appeared in *The New York Times*, May 4, 1895:

FELL DEAD AFTER HIS SPEECH

Edward Burrough, Road Commissioner of New-Jersey, Died at a Reunion of Veterans.

TRENTON, N. J. May 3.—Edward Burrough, State Road Commissioner and a prominent man in agricultural circles, fell dead this afternoon after delivering a patriotic speech to the veterans of the Twenty-third New-Jersey Volunteers, who were holding their annual reunion on Gen. E. Burd Grubb's lawn, at Edgewater Park. The cause of death was brain exhaustion. The reunion was abruptly brought to a close.

Don't let this happen to you. Don't "fall dead" after your speech due to "brain exhaustion." Maintain your mental edge as you shake hands and mingle with the crowd. Maintain your mental edge until the very last person departs. Maintain your mental edge until the last thank-you note goes off in the mail.

Then sit back and relax. Go to the beach. Or go fishing. You've earned a short break—until it's time for your *next* speech!

In the next chapter, we'll talk about how to take your public speaking game to the next level—and how to transform your communication ability into a rewarding and satisfying profession.

8

Take It to the Next Level

Comstock

One of my most memorable nights of my life was the Washington Speakers Bureau 25th Anniversary Gala in June 2005. It was a mega-event, hosted by one of the most prestigious speaker's agencies in the world, featuring all of their top-tier speakers: Lou Holtz, Rudy Giuliani, Tom Peters, Joe Theismann, Carly Fiorina, Madeleine Albright, Colin Powell, and others. I was in speakers heaven!

After the formal event, I went to the dessert table. As I reached for a chocolate éclair, I saw a hand go after the same éclair. I looked up—and there was Colin Powell. At that point, General Powell was part of a group trying to buy the Washington Nationals baseball team. I introduced myself and told him that my son Bobby was a manager in the Nationals farm system. That piqued his curiosity.

"General Powell," I said, "my son is a young leader in professional baseball. What advice would you give him?"

He said, "Tell him, first, 'Take care of the troops.' Second, 'Keep your mouth shut, and do your job.'" He started to walk away, then he stopped, looked at me over his shoulder and added, "And tell him, 'Don't worry about your next job.'"

And then he was gone into the night.

I quickly grabbed a napkin from the dessert table, pulled out my pen, and wrote down what General Powell had told me, so that I could pass it along to my son Bobby.

You never know who you might run into on the speaking trail. And you never know what you might learn. My conversation with General Powell—a distinguished leader who has served four presidents (Reagan, Bush 41, Clinton, and Bush 43)—was only made possible because, like him, I am a professional speaker and a client of the Washington Speakers Bureau.

If you're serious about public speaking, than you must ask yourself, "How far can I go? How high can I rise? Could I build a speaking business and become a *professional* public speaker? And what would I have to do to take myself and my speaking career to the next level?"

These are the questions we will answer in this chapter.

The Agencies and Bureaus That Control the Industry

Not everyone wants or needs to become a professional speaker. But for many of the people reading this book, the time will come when your speaking career begins to accelerate. You'll realize that there's an increasing demand for your message. You'll sense your confidence growing. You'll think, "I can *do* this! And I *like* doing this!"

If you can envision yourself becoming a professional speaker, it's time to consider signing with one or more speaker's agencies or bureaus. These organizations are a fact of life in the speaking world. In fact, I would say that 90 percent of my bookings over the past two decades have come through agencies. There are dozens of excellent agencies in North America, and there are a handful of agencies that dominate the field. The top agencies in the world include the aforementioned Washington Speakers Bureau in Alexandria, Virginia; Leading Authorities in Washington, D.C.; Keppler Speakers in Arlington, Virginia; Premiere Speakers Bureau in Franklin, Tennessee; and Gail Davis & Associates in Dallas, Texas.

Once you achieve a certain level of success, it's important to build a relationship with a speaking agency. These agencies can produce a lot of bookings for you and keep you working steadily. Agencies usually take a commission of 15 to 20 percent—and they earn it, because of the high-paying work they can bring you.

There's one important key to working with speaking agencies: You must have a good video that shows you in action in front of an audience. A substantial percentage of speakers are booked primarily, if not exclusively, on the basis of their videos. There was a time when you'd have to ship an audition video in the form of a bulky VHS videocassette. Meeting planners would have to pop that tape into a VCR and watch you in action.

Today, this is all done over the Internet. Meeting planners can go to a website and pull down two or three minutes of video to see you and several other speakers in action. Within minutes, they can make a decision as to whether you will make it to the finals. They might eliminate you or send you on to the next level in the matter of minutes. This is a highly competitive enterprise, and your video needs to show you to your best advantage, so it's best to have your video recorded and edited by a professional videographer. This investment in your speaking career will pay rich dividends over the years. Video is an important tool for marketing yourself and promoting your speaking brand.

Whenever you have a speaking engagement, make sure someone is recording it (if possible). Select a good three- to eight-minute clip that shows you at your inspirational best, wowing the crowd. In fact, it wouldn't hurt to include a few crowd shots showing smiling audience members hanging on every word!

Whenever I give a speech and I know the organization is recording the event, I ask for a copy. I have also hired videographers to record me at different events. I've put together a package with photos, interviews, endorsements from people who have hired me, and video clips, all of which can be accessed at my website: www.patwilliamsmotivate.com. Much of this material is also available on the websites of the speaking agencies I've worked with.

The speaking agencies control the highest levels of the public speaking industry. If you catch the eye of an agency and they like what you do, they can promote you to conventions and meeting planners—and they can absolutely change your life.

I have never been comfortable booking and negotiating speaking appearances on my own. It's awkward if someone calls you and asks, "What do you charge?" I think it diminishes the speaker when he does his own negotiating. So I like having the speaking agency handle the negotiations for me. For bookings that do not come through agencies, I have an associate who handles my bookings. Andrew Herdliska, my publicity specialist at the Orlando Magic, does all the negotiating for me. He takes care of the dates, the fee, and the travel arrangements. My job is to show up and speak. It's a great arrangement.

If you don't have an assistant, you could hire your spouse or one of your grown children to help you. This way, your speaking business could become a family business. Sometimes a wife, son, or daughter can be a much tougher negotiator than you ever could be—and the callers don't even have to know they are speaking to a relative.

The Speaking-Writing Synergy

Synergy may be defined as the effect of two forces being joined together so that their energy is not just *added* together, but *multiplied*. When synergy takes place, the power of the whole exceeds the sum of its parts.

The late futurist R. Buckminster Fuller used an analogy to explain the power of synergy: One of the strongest metals available today is chrome-nickel steel. Its primary ingredients are iron (tensile strength: 60,000 pounds per square inch), chromium (70,000 psi), and nickel (80,000 psi). If you add their tensile strength together, you get 210,000 psi. But when you create a chrome-nickel steel alloy, the result is a metal with 350,000 psi tensile strength. The strength of chrome-nickel steel is greater than the sum of its parts—and it makes possible the jet engines that power our airliners and military jets.

There is also a synergy between speaking and writing. When you're on the speaking circuit, and you have a book to sell, your speaking will magnify the sales of your book, and your book will enable you to get many more speaking engagements. Speaking and writing feed each other. They synergize each other. When you put a speaking career and a writing career together, the whole exceeds the sum of its parts.

So, as you climb the ladder of speaking success, at some point you should think about writing a book. The moment you have a book published, you become an expert on that topic. There's something about a book that tells people: "This person is knowledgeable. This person has mastered his field." And when you are considered an expert in a given field, people want to hear what you have to say. You'll take cartons of books to the event, and you'll have an opportunity to sign and sell them after your talk.

I often meet people who are struggling to build a public speaking business. They are excellent speakers and they have an excellent message. They know how to please and motivate an audience. But they are just not getting as many bookings as they need in order to make a go of it. So they ask me for advice. I always tell them, "Write a book." When you become an author, you take your game to a whole new level.

Obviously, writing a book isn't easy. When I tell people, "Write a book," they often look as if I had just told them to flap their wings and fly to the moon. "But I don't know the first thing about writing a book," they say. That's fine. If you need a writing partner, a professional wordsmith, then find someone who has a track record as a writer. Offer that person a sufficient amount of money (pay them half to start, and half on completion—don't pay it all up front), and get your book written. You can't get your book published until it is written.

"Write the *whole* book?" they ask.

"Yes," I reply, "write the *whole* book!"

"Well, how do I get it published?"

Let's be candid. The odds of you—an unknown first-time author—persuading a traditional publisher to take on your book are very slim. I hate to tell you that and you hate to hear it, but I'm giving it to you straight. And I say this as an author who has published more than 70 books with traditional publishers.

But I have good news for you. Due to changes in technology, the publishing world is changing rapidly. Today there are all sorts of alternatives to traditional publishing. When people ask me, "How can I get my book published?," I tell them about my friend Adam Witty with Advantage Media Group (www.advantagefamily.com), a subsidy publishing house in South Carolina. The principle difference between a traditional house and a subsidy publishing house is that traditional houses publish books at their own expense. In the subsidy publishing world, authors pay the publisher and subsidize the publication of their books.

You can choose from a number of subsidy houses, including Intermedia Publishing Group (www.intermediapub.com/), AuthorHouse (www.authorhouse.com), iUniverse (www.iuniverse.com), Xlibris (www.xlibris.com), and Xulon (www.xulonpress.com). I haven't had any personal experience with these other companies, but I have published six books with Advantage Media Group, and I can tell you that Advantage gets my books into print faster than any traditional publisher. They make these books available in bookstores and on Amazon.com as quality paperbacks and as e-books for Kindle and other electronic readers. The people at Advantage will explain how to publish and promote your book, and they can provide professional marketing resources for a separate charge. Within a few months, you can have your published book in your hands, ready to promote.

Compare this with the old process of landing a literary agent, having your book passed around to different publishers, and going through rejection after rejection. If it is ever accepted for publication, you must wait 9 to 18 months for the book to go through editing and production to finally emerge as a published book. The odds against landing a traditional publisher, or even landing a literary agent, are staggering. Why put yourself through that?

Instead, write the book (or pay a competent professional to write it with you), then pay a subsidy publisher to put your book into print. Then use your book to leverage your speaking career. Once you are an author, you are an expert—and you are well on your way to a full-time public speaking career.

Always keep a case or two of books in the trunk of your car. Wherever you go, if you have a chance to speak, you can set up a table in the back of the room and sell books. This is the perfect way to engage with your audience after your speech. You can sit down and chat with people and personalize their books—and they will come away, book in hand, feeling they have a piece of this experience that they can keep forever. They will continue to relive that experience as they read your book. It's a personal memento from you, and it adds a wonderful touch to your speaking career.

When you sell and sign books, it's important to have an assistant who handles the money. This leaves you free to interact with your audience. Frankly, it doesn't look good for you to handle money. Whether the assistant is someone who goes with you to all your speaking engagements, or someone provided by the event organizers, it's best to have help at your book table. Your assistant will help you keep the line moving. If the line gets backed up and people have to wait a long time, they'll get discouraged and leave empty-handed.

I recommend you price your book at a round number, such as $10 or $15. If there is sales tax, pay the tax yourself and make the transaction easy on your customer. Personally, I don't accept credit cards—just cash and checks. However, today's wireless communication technology enables you to swipe credit cards with your iPhone®, BlackBerry®, or other smartphone devices, so you may want to consider accepting credit cards at your book table.

A Life of Adventure

While this book was being written, I had an interesting experience at Southeastern University, a small Christian college in Lakeland, Florida. The university conducts an annual Leadership Week, which is promoted to the public. Leadership guru Ken Blanchard was one of the scheduled speakers. When Ken had to cancel, the organizers of the event asked me to step in and replace him. So I went to the campus on a Tuesday to give my talk.

While I was there, I was greeted by Dan Cathy, the president of the Chick-fil-A restaurant chain, who was also speaking at the event. He handed me a brochure for the Leadership Week, and I was amazed at the lineup of speakers. Billy Graham's son, Franklin Graham, was the featured speaker the next day. Super Bowl-winning quarterback (and *Dancing With the Stars* contestant) Kurt Warner would speak after lunch. Condoleezza Rice was scheduled for Thursday afternoon, and her former boss, George W. Bush, would speak on Friday. David Gergen, former advisor to four U.S. presidents, was also on the docket, along with a number of other business leaders and experts.

Looking at that brochure, I thought, "Wow! All of these great leaders will be right here in Lakeland. This is as star-studded a leadership cast as I've ever seen. People come here from all along the Eastern Seaboard to hear them speak—and I get to be a part of it!" As I said, you never know who you might encounter on the speaking trail. It's a life of adventure, and you cross paths with the most fascinating people.

Well, at this point, I think you're ready to graduate from the Pat Williams College of Speaking Knowledge and go for your post-grad degree. In the next chapter, I am going to take you through the Alfonso Castaneira Grad School of Public Speaking.

9

The Alfonso Castaneira Graduate School of Public Speaking

Digital Vision

My friend Scott Crites used to book speakers for his organization of business leaders. Always on the lookout for new talent, he called me one day and said, "Pat, I've met a fellow over in the Tampa area, Alfonso Castaneira. He's a speaker and a speaking coach, and I'd appreciate it if you would check him out for me. I would value your opinion of his skills as a speaking coach."

So I contacted Alfonso and told him I'd like to meet him. I had a speaking engagement in Port Charlotte, south of Tampa, and I asked if he could meet me there. Alfonso drove to the event, set up a video camera, and recorded my speech. Afterwards, we sat down together in front of a TV monitor and watched my presentation.

"May I be candid?" he asked at one point.

"Please do!" said I. "Bring it on!"

I didn't want Alfonso to tiptoe around my feelings. I wanted him to treat me as a professional, as a true student of the craft, someone who is focused on continual learning, growth, and improvement. So Alfonso didn't spare my feelings. Instead, he gave me a number of extremely helpful pointers that I had never heard from other speaking coaches. I was eager to implement those insights, and I came away very impressed with Alfonso Castaneira.

Returning to Orlando, I called Scott and said, "This guy is good! He has a personable manner, and he really knows the speaking business."

That was my introduction to Alfonso Castaneira, and over the years I have kept in touch with him. Whenever I speak in his area, he comes to hear me and always has a piece of valuable advice to share with me. That's what I mean by the "Alfonso Castaneira Graduate School of Public Speaking." I have grown so much under his tutelage, and now, with his permission, I will share some of his most practical and transformative insights with you.

Alfonso's Lesson #1: Use video feedback.

If the top golfers in the world need putting coaches and stroke coaches, if the best baseball players in the world have hitting instructors, if the best pitchers have pitching gurus who help them go from great to even greater, doesn't it make sense for speakers, at every level from novice to virtuoso, to have speech coaches? It sure makes sense to me.

Whenever possible, I try to have a friend, preferably a speaking professional, in the audience to give me feedback and a reality check. And when I say "friend," I mean someone who cares enough to give it to me straight, without sparing my feelings. I always consider it a privilege when that friend is Alfonso himself. Every time he monitors one of my talks, he gives me a list of improvements I could make.

One of the first lessons I learned from Alfonso is the power of video feedback. Video enables you to see yourself exactly as audiences see you. It's objective. It's factual. When you see yourself on video, you can't argue with what you see and hear. Video reveals your communicating strengths, so that you can build on them. And video reveals your communicating weaknesses, so that you can eliminate them.

I constantly used video feedback to improve my communicating skills. Whenever I speak, I get a video of my presentation, and I watch it with a critical eye, usually with a friend or a speaking coach alongside me. I always want a fresh view of how I did and perspective on what I can do better.

Yes, I know it's painful to see yourself on video. You'll wince, you'll hide your eyes, and you'll ask, "Does my voice *really* sound like that?" You'll hate the mistakes you make, the occasional stammer or flubbed word. But that's how you learn! That's how you grow and improve! You can't overcome bad communication habits until you know what they are, so face the truth without flinching.

Alfonso's Lesson #2: Make your movements match your message.

Everything you do and say as a speaker must be congruent. This means that your words, your tone of voice, your facial expression, your gestures, and your body language must all be in agreement. People often assume, "I said the words, so my audience got my message." That's not always true. Every message has both verbal and nonverbal content. Your words may mean one thing, but if your tone of voice, your body language, and you're gestures don't match your words, then your message will be canceled out. In fact, if your verbal message and your nonverbal message don't match, your audience may judge you to be insincere or deceptive. So let's talk about movement.

Many public speakers have a difficult time learning to coordinate their hand gestures with their words. They fan and chop the air in a way that is totally unsynchronized with what they are saying, and these chaotic gestures undermine their message. Learning to coordinate your gestures with your words is a valuable skill that's well worth learning. Properly used, your hands can give emphasis, power, and punctuation to your spoken words. Video feedback will show you when your gestures and words are synchronized— and when they are out of sync. This information will help you to be more conscious of your gestures so you can improve your communicating performance.

"Remember," Alfonso told me, "from the moment you step onto the stage, the audience is evaluating you. So when you move onto the stage, step up with energy, a dynamic stride, and a confident smile. Don't just make a good first impression. Make an *impact*! Let your audience know by the way you square your shoulders and look them in the eye that you are bringing them a message that will change their lives."

Alfonso is right. If you step onto the stage in a hesitant way, if you seem unsure of yourself or your message, if you seem intimidated by the audience or the setting, then you are in for a rough time. Make sure the audience feels your confidence, your belief in your message. Don't take it too far; don't swagger. Don't come across as arrogant or condescending. Just be yourself—the best, most confident self you can be.

One of the most crucial decisions you will make as a speaker is where you will stand to deliver your talk. At the beginning of my speaking career, I always clung to the lectern. I had my notes there. I could grip the lectern, and that gave me something to do with my hands. The lectern was my crutch.

For the beginning speaker, the lectern provides a psychological safety barrier against the audience—and that's exactly the problem with the lectern! The audience senses that you want distance between yourself and them. The lectern tells the audience that you're uncomfortable in front of them. It even tells them that you're *afraid* of them. As motivational speaker Jay Carty once told me, "Remove all that stands between you and the audience. No lectern, no distance—sometimes I even take my glasses off. I want no barriers between the audience and me."

A few years into my speaking career, I began to see the lectern as a blockage between myself and the audience. So my first bold move was to come out from behind the lectern and stand alongside it, possibly leaning on it. Oh yes, it was still my crutch, my security blanket. If I began to feel uncomfortable beside the lectern, I could always retreat behind it, check my notes, and shield myself from the audience once more.

That first tentative move to free myself from the safety (and tyranny) of the lectern felt like a bold step forward. Looking back, I realize I was only taking baby steps toward the freedom of being a confident communicator. In time, I worked up the courage to move away from the lectern and stand up on the stage a little closer to the audience. I no longer relied on my notes, and my confidence grew as I experienced increasing success away from the lectern.

This led to my next bold move, which was to come down the steps and deliver my talk at eye level with the audience, right in front of the first row. I thought I had hit the jackpot.

But then, in 1996, America was introduced to the "Elizabeth Dole Stroll" (see Chapter 2). The wife of presidential candidate Bob Dole gave an electrifying speech at the Republican National Convention while strolling around the floor, without notes or teleprompter, delivering a speech that was often described as reminiscent of Oprah Winfrey. When I saw that speech, I was stunned. I had never seen anything like it! A whole new approach to public speaking opened up for me. I wanted the Elizabeth Dole Stroll to be the Pat Williams Stroll!

That became my goal. The most radical and transformative step I took as a public speaker was the step of going out into the crowd, meeting people eye-to-eye, speaking to them as individuals, even checking their name tag and addressing them by their first name. I interacted with them, directed questions at individuals, and incorporated their answers into my talk.

You may not feel ready to take the Elizabeth Dole Stroll. That's okay. But your goal as a speaker should be to free yourself from the disabling crutch of the lectern. Your goal should be to gain the confidence to be truly *free* as a public speaker, so you can move closer to your audience. Instead of delivering a speech, you can have a *conversation* with your listeners. And to have a conversation, you must be free to *move*.

One question people often ask me is: "What do I do with my hands?" That is every speaker's dilemma, especially at the beginning. Let me tell you, first of all, do not put them in your pockets. Don't hide them, and don't clasp them in front of you like a fig leaf. Your hands are among your greatest assets when you speak, so use them! They should be as expressive as your face. Make big, bold gestures with your hands. Use them to add emphasis to your words. Hammer your point home with your hands.

What about your movements on the stage? Should you move around on the stage or stay in one place? It depends on the room. Alfonso explained it to me this way: "If you're in a big hall, such as a theater or large lecture hall, you can't roam around as you would in a medium-sized conference room or fireplace room. Why? Because if you walk around on the stage of a large-capacity venue, you look like an ant. And if there are big video screens behind you, your movements will only magnify the problem. That's because the cameras will constantly try to track with you as you move around the stage. Camera motion is distracting and causes you to look frenzied and out of control."

Alfonso is right. In a large venue, you have to stay on the stage in one place in order to show up well on the screens. I learned this lesson the hard way.

I was in a huge hall, speaking to an audience of about 800 people. I decided to come down on eye level with the audience. I later received a critique from the organizers of the event, and they were *not* happy. I may have made a good impression on the people in the first few rows, but most of the audience was unable to see me. The lighting had been carefully set up to illuminate a speaker on the stage, but there was no lighting for the audience area. So when I went out to the audience, I was in semi-darkness. I didn't show up well on the screens, and people in the audience complained that they couldn't see me and couldn't hear me very well.

In a smaller, more intimate setting, where the audience is closer and there are no lighting or sound problems to deal with, the Elizabeth Dole Stroll works very well. And your goal should be to break free of the lectern and connect with your audience. But in a large hall, you must consider issues of lighting and sound quality.

Alfonso also gave me some tips on what to do when I move out into the crowd. "Stop at a table," he said. "Talk to one person individually. If that person has a name tag, use that person's first name. Engage him in a one-on-one conversation. Put your hand on his shoulder. That small act of touching one person in the audience creates a human connection with the entire audience. People notice, even if only at a subliminal level. And by personalizing one individual, you personalize the whole room. When you use one person's name, everyone in the room feels you've used his or her name. Do it, but don't overdo it or it will seem forced and insincere."

I've taken Alfonso's advice, and I can tell you that this is a powerful way of connecting with the audience. When you use the first name of someone in the audience, that person sits straight up in the chair, and so does the entire audience. You have the undivided attention of everyone in the room. It's electrifying. Try it, and you'll be amazed at how close you feel to everyone in the room.

Alfonso's Lesson #3: Start and end on time.

At your pre-call, the event planner told you when you should start and when you should finish. That's not a goal; that's an expectation. You have an obligation to start and finish on time. Your hosts have many other activities scheduled in addition to your speech. If you blow right past your closing time, you create a bad impression that will eventually become a bad reputation. "Don't make the event planner have to wave at you from the back of the room," Alfonso says. "Stick to your timeline."

Beginning and ending on time takes preparation. It means that, when you are practicing your speech in the days and weeks before the event, you have to time it out, allow extra time for questions and interruptions, and know exactly where you have to be in your outline at the halfway mark, the three-quarter mark, and during the final ten minutes. And when your time is up, you're done.

Don't overstay your welcome—or your audience's attention span. If you run overtime in your rehearsals, don't try to talk faster. Cut some material so you can maintain a relaxed and comfortable speaking pace. In the public speaking world, less is often more.

If you tend to lose track of the time while you speak, have a friend or assistant sit in the front row with cards that read: "15 Minutes," "10 Minutes," "5 Minutes," and "Finish!" Make sure you pace your talk so you don't have to cram in your last five points in two minutes. The audience knows when you're rushing through the material, and they'll feel cheated if you don't give them a complete presentation of your final points. When your pace is even and measured, you come across as authoritative and in command of your material. When you are scrambling to catch up, you look scattered and incompetent.

Your final points are often your most important material—your knockout punch. If you plan your speech poorly, you may end up undermining the very material that you meant to underscore.

Throughout your talk, be clear and concise. Speak in simple, easy-to-follow sentences. Stick to your point, underscore your point, drive your point home, and make it unforgettable.

Alfonso's Lesson #4: Become an actor.

Alfonso Castaneira revolutionized the way I look at storytelling in speeches. "Don't just *tell* a story," he said. "*Become* the story. Act the story out. Bring it to life right before their eyes. Instead of saying, 'He said such-and-such,' and, 'She said so-and-so,' *become* those two characters. Speak his dialogue, then speak her dialogue. Suddenly your speech is no longer a speech. It's a play, it's a movie, and your audience is drawn right into the action. It's so much more effective."

He suggested that, in my leadership talk, I should actually portray some of the leaders I talk about. Instead of merely quoting from John F. Kennedy's inaugural address, why not adopt his facial expressions, his mannerisms, and his Boston accent as I speak the lines: "Let the word go forth that the torch has been passed to a new generation of Americans…. Ask not what your country can do for you. Ask what you can do for your country." Okay, my accent is more of a cheesy Mayor Quimby from *The Simpsons* than authentic JFK, but somehow it seems to work.

Alfonso's point is that a speaker should become not just a storyteller, but an actor. When you actually become the people you tell about, your audience members come away feeling they have had an actual encounter with your characters. Your listeners witness the action and feel the emotions. Their imaginations fill in any missing details, and the whole experience becomes amazingly real.

The story is told of novelist Herman Melville, the author of *Moby Dick*, who was a good friend of fellow novelist Nathaniel Hawthorne. After returning from a trip to the South Seas, Melville visited Hawthorne and his wife in their Concord, Massachusetts, home. During the visit, Melville told the Hawthornes about a violent fight he had witnessed in which a Polynesian warrior had battled several foes with a wooden club. As he described the drama, Melville acted out the part of the club-wielding warrior, swinging about, seeming to break enemy limbs and bash enemy heads with every stroke.

Later, after Melville left, Mrs. Hawthorne remembered that their friend had gone out the door without his club. Mr. and Mrs. Hawthorne proceeded to search their house but they could not find Melville's club anywhere. The next day, they saw Herman Melville in town, and they asked what he had done with the club.

"Club?" Melville asked, perplexed. "I had no club."

It turned out that Melville had acted out his story so convincingly that the Hawthorne's *thought* they had seen a club in his hands. The club had been nothing but a figment of their imaginations.

You and I have the same ability to ignite the imaginations of our audiences. Don't just tell stories. *Become* your stories. Make your stories *live* in the imagination of your audience.

Alfonso's Lesson #5: Obey the 20-minute rule.

Alfonso's 20-minute rule is very simple: Make sure you get the audience moving every 20 minutes. If you give a 60-minute talk, introduce some audience movement at the 20-minute mark and the 40-minute mark. If you don't, your audience will lose focus—and you'll lose your audience.

What kind of movement are we talking about? Well, you could have your audience stand and stretch at the 20-minute mark, then have them switch chairs at the 40-minute mark. You might have them give a shoulder massage to the person next to them (first the one to their right, then the one to their left). Whenever possible, tie the movement to the theme of your talk. For example, when I give my talk on Walt Disney, I have the audience draw a mouse and write the word "stick-to-it-ivity" under the mouse (that was Walt's word for perseverance—the character quality he needed in order to bring Mickey Mouse to the motion picture screen).

Alfonso also suggested, "Why don't you have the crowd do The Wave around the room? People love doing The Wave at games, and they'd enjoy it as a break during a speech." I haven't tried that yet, but I plan to.

These actions will give your audience a sense that you are giving three 20-minute talks instead of one hour-long talk. When you reset the clock every 20 minutes, you give your audience a moment of refreshment—and they are ready to listen for another 20 minutes. An audience may struggle to stay awake through a 60-minute speech, but any listener can give attention to a speaker for 20 minutes. If you obey the 20-minute rule, you will never lose your audience.

Alfonso's Lesson #6: Make the abstract tangible.

A speech is nothing but words, vibrations on the air—*until* you find a way to make abstract ideas tangible and memorable to your audience. One way to do this is through tangible rewards. For example, you might ask the audience, "What one point did I make today that will change your life tomorrow?" When someone in the audience puts up a hand and answers your question, give that person a signed book or some other memento as a reward. Now your concept is no longer just words on air; it has been translated into a tangible reward.

Alfonso also suggested a way to reward people for coming to your talk. Tape your business card to the underside of one of the chairs. During a "stretch break," have the audience check their chairs for the business card. Whoever is sitting in the "lucky chair" gets a signed book or other prize. People love giveaways. It's fun, and it keeps them engaged, because they never know what you might pull out of a hat next.

One day, when Alfonso was in the audience to critique my speech, I said to the audience, "What I'm going to say right now is a take-home point. If you walk out of here today and forget everything else I say, make sure you remember this point, and take it home with you." Then I picked up a cloth napkin from the table, raised in over my head, and twirled it around and around the way Pittsburgh Steelers fans twirl their Terrible Towels. "This twirling napkin indicates a take-home point."

After my speech, Alfonso came up to me and said, "Twirling that napkin was a good idea. But next time, involve the whole audience. Have *everyone in the audience* pick up their napkins and twirl them overhead when you make a take-home point. Imagine a whole roomful of twirling napkins. That will *really* make your point memorable."

That's how Alfonso thinks. He knows a good idea when he sees one, and he usually knows a way to make it even better.

Alfonso's Lesson #7: Maintain your passion and energy.

Alfonso continually underscores this principle. When you get up to speak, you are not merely communicating information. You are communicating your *passion* for your subject. So you must do whatever it takes to keep yourself emotionally charged up before, during, and even after you speak. You must maintain an edge of emotional intensity throughout the entire time you're with your audience.

Speaking is much like an athletic event. Athletes don't have good days every single day. Some days they'd rather stay home and not go to the ballpark, the track, the tennis court, or the golf course. But just as an athlete can't afford a down day, neither can a speaker. You have to be ready whenever you are called upon to stand and communicate. You must summon all the passion within you and use it to deliver your best performance.

Leadership expert Patrick Lencioni once explained it to me this way: "Let your passion run wild. Your audience will forgive many of your faults as long as you are passionate." And business speaker Tom Peters told me, "Never step onto the stage unless you are exuding passion. That's what you're selling."

If you give 99 great speeches and one lackluster speech, I guarantee that the one poor speech will follow you and hurt your reputation. One bad report will make a speaking agency wary of you. Whether you feel like it or not, always be ready to dig down and summon up the passion within. Always find a way to deliver a sparkling performance.

Alfonso's Lesson #8: Seek continual feedback.

Your final lesson in the Alfonso Castaneira Graduate School of Public Speaking is simple and obvious (even though many speakers fail to heed it): Seek continual feedback. "Good enough" is never good enough. You can always improve, always grow, and always learn.

I was recently talking to a meeting planner, and I asked her what the people in her organization liked and disliked in the speakers they hired for their events. What makes a speaker memorable? And what makes you wish you could forget a certain speaker?

She didn't even have to think about the answer. She had her answer ready because the people in her organization had recently considered a number of speakers, and they had talked about the pluses and minuses of each one.

"First," she said, "my people like to hear personal experiences. They like to hear a speaker talk about their own experiences, not just stories and ideas out of books. Memorable speakers bring a wealth of personal stories to share. Second, my people like to receive practical tips, not just theories. Third, my people like to listen to a speaker who is funny, who communicates with a good sense of humor. Fourth, my people like a speaker who understands our industry, makes reference to our specific problems and issues, and speaks our language. We want to know that you took the time to craft a message that is specifically targeted at our needs."

And what did her organization dislike about some speakers? "First, we don't like presentations that are preachy, that scold us and tell us that we are wrong. We know we have problems. We want the speaker to tell us how to solve our problems—but without scolding or judging us. Second, we don't like speakers who yell. Let's have a conversation. Some speakers think that they can fire us up by shouting at us, but it's really offensive and off-putting. Third, we don't like speakers with a negative tone. Give us optimism. Give us hope. Give us good news. Motivate us and recharge our batteries. Negative talk just leaves us drained. Fourth, we don't like speakers who are aloof and condescending. We want to know that you care about us and that you want us to succeed."

That was valuable feedback. Often, as I am preparing to give my next speech, I think about the feedback I've received over the years. It inspires and motivates me to deliver what my audience needs and wants.

In January 1996, I was scheduled to speak at a Saturday luncheon in New York. There was a huge snowstorm in New York City at the time. I was scheduled to fly back to Orlando Saturday night and run my first marathon—the Disney Marathon—the following day.

I had always wanted to have one of my speeches critiqued by Peggy Noonan, the author and speechwriter who worked for CBS News anchorman Dan Rather in the 1970s and for the Reagan White House in the 1980s. A mutual friend had given me Peggy's phone number, so I called her when I arrived in New York on Friday. I introduced myself and told her I was speaking at a luncheon the next day, and I'd be honored if she'd come and critique my talk.

"I can't promise I'll be there," she told me, "but I'll try." I didn't think she'd come.

The next day, as I was about five minutes into my speech, I glanced at the back of the room and saw a woman in an overcoat come tip-toeing in, accompanied by an eight-year-old boy. She took a seat near the back row. I had seen Peggy Noonan on TV but had never met her, but I thought to myself, "That must be her!"

After I finished my talk, the woman and her son came up. I said, "You must be Peggy Noonan. Do you have to rush off? Could we grab a late lunch?"

And we did! We sat in the restaurant and had a marvelous chat. Her son was a bright and mature eight-year-old. They were both quite charming.

I asked Peggy for her critique of my speech, and she very graciously said, "There's nothing I can tell you about public speaking." Well, I'm sure there was, but I thanked her all the same. Peggy and I have talked by phone a few times since. I regularly read her column in the *Wall Street Journal* and am one of her biggest fans.

Alfonso has drilled it into me: We can always grow, always improve—and we should constantly ask for critiques and feedback, every time we speak. We may not always get the criticism we ask for. In fact, we may just get a bouquet of lovely compliments instead—and I'll gladly take that, too!

So that's the Alfonso Castaneira Graduate School of Public Speaking. I keep his pointers taped to my credenza, I review them frequently, and I add to them every time he critiques one of my speeches. (If you'd like to receive personal training from Alfonso himself, I've listed his contact information in the back of this book.)

In the next chapter, we'll pull all the principles of this book together into a grand conclusion. So what are we waiting for? Let's go!

10

How Far Do You Want to Go?

Jupiterimages

In October 1996, I took part in the 27th running of the Marine Corps Marathon in Washington, D.C. The race began in Arlington, Virginia, near the Marine Corps War Memorial with its majestic statue of the flag raising on Iwo Jima. The course wound its way through our nation's capital, past all the stately monuments to Washington, Lincoln, and Jefferson. That was only the third marathon I had run, and it was an exhilarating experience.

I had an equally inspiring experience later that evening when I had dinner with George McGovern, the former senator from South Dakota who ran unsuccessfully against Richard Nixon in 1972. Senator McGovern is a humble man and a fascinating dinner companion. He told me stories about his many famous friends (including JFK, RFK, LBJ, and HHH), and a few of his political opponents. He even had some fascinating stories to tell about an eager young man he hired as his Texas state campaign director, a 26-year-old up-and-comer named Bill Clinton.

A few years later, I reconnected with Senator McGovern and interviewed him for my book *Coaching Your Kids to Be Leaders*. In that interview, I discovered that Senator McGovern learned early in life that public speaking is the key that unlocks the door to leadership. His speaking ability enabled him to be elected president of his class in college, and he won a statewide speaking contest with a speech called "My Brother's Keeper."

As a B-24 bomber pilot in World War II, McGovern flew 35 combat missions over Europe. On his final mission—a raid on the heavily defended oil and ammunition depots at Linz, Austria—McGovern and his crew braved flak so thick that it blew more than a hundred holes in the fuselage and wings of his aircraft. His waist gunner was badly wounded and his flight engineer completely paralyzed by fright. The plane's hydraulic system was shot away and one engine knocked out. McGovern had to improvise a new way of landing the plane. He brought it down steep and fast, had two crewmen deploy parachutes from the rear of the plane to create drag, and ordered the rest of the crew to huddle in the tail section to keep the plane's nose up. The result was a barely controlled crash into a ditch—but McGovern brought everyone through alive.[1]

McGovern was elected to the Senate from South Dakota in 1962, then reelected in 1968 and 1974. He credits his speaking ability for his years of successful leadership in Washington, D.C. "My high school English teacher told me I had a talent in public speaking," Senator McGovern told me. "She introduced me to the high school debate coach. Debating transformed me from a somewhat shy and reticent student to a more confident and persuasive public speaker.

"The Roman orator Marcus Fabius Quintilian once defined an orator as 'a good man speaking well.' You must first become a good man or a good woman before you are worth listening to as a speaker. It's the same way with other activities: A good teacher is a good person teaching well. A good coach is a good person coaching well. A good parent is a good person parenting well. I encourage people, especially young people, to become a good person first, then a good speaker. Then use that ability to help others be better people. The life well lived is its own reward."

Those are wise words from a man who has lived his life well, spoken well, and used his skills as a public speaker to achieve his party's nomination for president of the United States.

How far will *your* speaking skills take *you*? How far do you want to go?

Using Words to Change the World

If you look at the roster of the great leaders of the world, you'll see that most achieved their leadership goals through the power of public speaking. Yet if you look more closely, you'll notice that many of those great public speakers had very little natural talent as communicators. Many of them started with disabilities rather than abilities, and they worked hard to overcome their deficiencies in order to achieve leadership greatness.

Take, for example, the Old Testament leader Moses. In Exodus 4:10, when God called Moses to lead the Israelites out of Egypt, Moses objected, saying, "I have never been eloquent ... . I am slow of speech and tongue."[2] Some historians suggest that Moses had a speech impediment. Whether he had an actual impediment or was simply lacking in confidence, it's clear that Moses was no silver-tongued orator. Yet today he is revered as one of history's greatest leaders—and greatest speakers. His speeches before Pharaoh and before the people of Israel are recorded in the Old Testament books of Exodus through Deuteronomy. He was a leader because he ultimately overcame his deficiencies to become a great speaker.

Demosthenes (384–322 B.C.) was one of the great statesman and public speakers of ancient Athens. His speeches have been recorded and preserved through the centuries as among the loftiest expressions of Greek political philosophy and culture. But Demosthenes, like Moses, was not a naturally gifted orator. In his youth, Demosthenes suffered from a serious speech impediment, which he overcame by practicing his diction with a mouth full of pebbles. How important were the speeches of Demosthenes to the life of ancient Greece? History records that his speeches rallied the people of Athens to take up arms and defend Greece from attack by Philip II and the Macedonian army.

Moses and Demosthenes were two great men who lived well, spoke well, and used their skills as public speakers to lead their people and save their nations from bondage. How far will *your* speaking skills take *you*? How far do you want to go?

My friend Richard E. Lapchick has been called "the Social Conscience of Sports" because of his dedication to using sports to solve social and racial problems in our culture. He is chairman of the DeVos Sport Business Management Program at the University of Central Florida, director of the National Consortium for Academics and

Sports, and the author of many books. Richard Lapchick is a leader because he is a public speaker. He once told me that his transformation as a speaker and a leader began when he was in high school:

"I realized as a returning 10th grade student that I had the ability to lead. I left home that summer thinking I was going to play basketball, but I ended up traveling in Europe instead. I was a different person when I came back. I told my fellow students about my experiences visiting Dachau, the Nazi concentration camp, and the tremendous impact it had on my life.

"I noticed that other students paid much more attention to me when I talked to them about serious issues. It was the first time I realized that I could discuss serious events and people would listen. During that same time, I also noticed the influence that leaders in the civil rights movement were having on the world. I was especially impacted by such leaders as Martin Luther King, Jr., Malcolm X, Cesar Chavez, Nelson Mandela, and Robert Kennedy. And every one of them was a great speaker.

"As a senior in high school, I was asked to give the salutatorian address at commencement. I was expected to simply greet the graduates and their families, then sit down. Having been to previous commencements, it was usually the least notable moment on those occasions. But I decided to do something a bit more memorable. I decided to talk about racism and the civil rights movement.

"That was in the late spring of 1963. The March on Washington was several months away, scheduled for the summer. There was a great deal of apprehension nationwide about what would happen. I talked about how the races could work together using the model of sports. My dad [Boston Celtics center Joe Lapchick] coached basketball, and my friend, Leroy Ellis, played for him. Leroy was a 6'11" All-American center, and he attended the commencement.

"I gave my talk, and the audience wasn't sure how to react until this big 6'11" center rose up above the crowd, giving me a standing ovation. Seconds later, the rest of the audience joined him on their feet, clapping. At that moment I understood that the power to speak is the power to influence—and the power to lead."

My friend Richard Lapchick is on a mission to transform our culture and heal the racial divisions in our world, using sports as a bridge to bring people together. He's a leader today because, as a young man, he made a decision to build and hone his speaking skills, and to use those skills to make the world a better place.

What will you do with *your* speaking skills? How far will they take you? How far do you want to go?

Great Words Produce Great Movements in History

I never cease to be amazed by the power of the spoken word, by the impact of a dynamic presentation. People the world over are fascinated by great speakers. The great movements of history have always come as a result of people who used their communication skills to speak out about the crucial issues of their time:

- Jonathan Edwards and George Whitefield and the Great Awakening
- The great orators of the American Revolution and the founding of the United States of America
- William Wilberforce and the end of the English slave trade
- Abraham Lincoln and the emancipation of the slaves
- Elizabeth Cady Stanton and women's suffrage
- Winston Churchill and victory in the Battle of Britain
- John F. Kennedy and the decision to go to the Moon
- Dr. Martin Luther King, Jr., and the civil rights movement
- Ronald Reagan's "tear down this wall" speech and the fall of the Berlin Wall

Almost every great movement in history has begun with great men and women communicating great ideas through the power of the spoken word.

While this book was being written, noted speaker Bruce Wilkinson, author of *The Prayer of Jabez*, came to speak at First Baptist Church, Orlando, over Saturday night and Sunday morning. With the power of his words alone, he shook that church to its foundation.

"You have a crisis right here in Orlando," he said. "You may think that the church is what goes on inside these walls. But the truth is that the ministry of this church is on the outside of these walls, not the inside. All around, you have a crisis of homelessness, of repossessed houses, of lost jobs, of families living in one-room hotel rooms. The task of the church is right here, all around you, in your neighborhood. What are you going to do about it?"

Bruce Wilkinson delivered this message in three services, speaking to a combined audience of about 10,000 people. When he was finished speaking, the congregation had anted up *$5.2 million to meet human needs in the Orlando community*. Wilkinson poured himself out to that congregation, and the people opened their hearts and their checkbooks in a way that has never happened before in that church. I know of one man who committed half a million dollars to the cause, right on the spot—and I don't think he came to church with any notion that he would do that.

With my own eyes that Sunday morning, I saw a great movement of human hearts—and it has become a life-changing movement throughout our community. That's the power of a public speaker who has lived his life well, who speaks well, and who uses his communication skills to achieve great things for God, for the community, and for people in need.

How far will *your* speaking skills take *you*? How far do you want to go?

The power of the spoken word can impact lives and families, move society in a new direction, alter the course of history, and transform the world. You have that world-changing power within your hands, between your ears, right on the tip of your tongue. In this book, I have laid out a game plan for you to study, apply, and put into practice. So take these principles and work hard at your craft. Take pride in your work. Remember, every time you get up to speak, you have the power to change the world, one heart, one mind at a time.

Following are the principles that you can take *right now* and implement in your speaking career. These are the keys to changing your life and your world:

- *Have a reason to speak.* What is your message? What qualifies you to speak on this subject? Why should people want to hear your talk? The answer to this question is the first vital element of your speech. Once you have a reason to speak, develop your signature speech—the message that you are passionate about, the message that defines you. Practice it, learn it, own it, and deliver it wherever and whenever you can.
- *Get organized.* The only confident, successful speaker is a prepared speaker. Preparation and organization are vital to your success as a communicator. Create a speech that is so well-structured and clearly organized that people in your audience can take good notes. Your ultimate goal is to have a speech that you can deliver anytime, anywhere, completely without notes.
- *Begin with a grand opening.* You have 15 seconds to win your audience over—or you are in for a difficult speech. Never open a speech with a weak opening of meaningless chatter. Begin with an attention-getting opening that rivets your audience.
- *Know where you're going.* Use the simple outline in Chapter 4 to create an effective, well-structured speech.
- *Connect with your listeners through humor and stories.* Audiences love to laugh, and they love a good story. Humor opens the minds of your listeners. Stories instruct, illuminate, and make your message unforgettable.
- *Finish strong!* A weak ending can ruin an otherwise great speech. Make sure your ending brings your listeners to their feet for a standing ovation.
- *Prepare yourself before you speak.* Use the power of the pre-call to get to know your audience. Don't be a recluse; meet and greet your hosts and make friends with your audience before you speak. Get plenty of sleep the night before you

speak, and avoid alcohol. Exercise your body and your voice for greater mental clarity. Do the pumpkin-raisin drill to limber up your face muscles. Don't neglect breakfast. Prepare yourself physically, mentally, and spiritually so you can give your best effort to your audience.

- *To take your speaking career to the next level, write a book and sign with a speakers bureau.* A book to sign and sell makes you an authority. A speakers agency will make you a star.
- *Seek out a speaking coach.* My coach, Alfonso Castaneira, has enabled me to greatly improve my speaking skills in a short period of time. Take Alfonso's advice: Use the power of video feedback. Start and end on time. Learn to match your movements to your message. Become an actor and act out your stories. Throughout your speech, maintain your passion and energy.

Finally, I wish you well in your public speaking career. In fact, I believe that speaking is more than just a career. Speaking is a *calling*. I hope that you will take up this challenge and use your speaking abilities to change the world for the better. The power to speak before an audience is the power to *transform the world* around you.

So I ask you one last time: How far do you want to go?

Endnotes

Chapter 1: A Reason to Speak

1. Richard Holmes, *In the Footsteps of Churchill* (New York: Basic, 2006), 40.

Chapter 2: Getting Organized

1. Jeralyn E. Merritt, "Jeanine Pirro's First Speech: The 32 Second Pause," TalkLeft. com, August 11, 2005, http://www.talkleft.com/story/2005/08/11/217/44699.
2. Eric Etheridge, "A President and His Teleprompter," NYTimes.com, March 26, 2009, http://opinionator.blogs.nytimes.com/2009/03/26/a-president-and-his-teleprompter/.
3. Ibid.
4. Ibid.
5. Ibid.
6. Alexander Burns, "Obama Gets Ahead of Prompter," Politico.com, April 27, 2009, http://www.politico.com/politico44/perm/0409/obama_gets_ahead_of_prompter_3813cbcb-1e4a-44c6-b1e7-26017e7b70c2.html.

Chapter 4: Know Where You're Going

1. Michael Reagan, *The New Reagan Revolution* (New York: St. Martin's Press, 2011), 159-162.

Chapter 5: "Let Me Tell You a Story …"

1. Dave Barry, "A Brush With Gardening," syndicated column, July 30, 1989, http://www.miamiherald.com/2011/04/17/2162152/a-brush-with-gardening.html.
2. Matthew 13:34, New International Version®. Copyright © 1973, 1978, 1984 by Biblica, Inc. All rights reserved worldwide. Used by permission.
3. Doris Kearns Goodwin, *Team of Rivals: The Political Genius of Abraham Lincoln* (New York: Simon & Schuster, 2005), 50.
4. Ibid., 50.
5. Ibid., 8, 150.

Chapter 7: Before You Speak—and After

1. Andy Williams, *Moon River and Me: A Memoir* (New York: Penguin, 2009), 287.
2. Cathy Lynn Grossman, "The Gospel of Billy Graham: Inclusion," *USA Today*, May 15, 2005, http://www.usatoday.com/news/religion/2005-05-15-graham-cover_x.htm.
3. Times staff, "Fell Dead After His Speech," *New York Times*, May 4, 1895, http://query.nytimes.com/mem/archive-free/pdf?res=FA0B17FF3B5D15738DDDAD0894DD405B8585F0D3.

Chapter 10: How Far Do You Want to Go?

1. Stephen E. Ambrose, *The Wild Blue: The Men and Boys Who Flew the B-24s Over Germany* (New York: Simon & Schuster, 2001), 241-245.
2. Exodus 4:10, New International Version.

About the Author

Pat Williams is the senior vice president of the NBA's Orlando Magic. As one of America's top motivational, inspirational, and humorous speakers, he has addressed thousands of executives in organizations ranging from Fortune 500 companies and national associations to universities and nonprofits. Clients include Allstate, American Express, Cisco, Coca-Cola, Disney, Honeywell, IBM, ING, Lockheed Martin, Nike, PriceWaterhouseCoopers, and Tyson Foods to name a few. Pat is also the author of over 70 books.

Pat served for seven years in the United States Army, spent seven years in the Philadelphia Phillies organization—two as a minor league catcher and five in the front office—and has also spent three years in the Minnesota Twins organization. Since 1968, he has been in the NBA as general manager for teams in Chicago, Atlanta, and Philadelphia—including the 1983 World Champion 76ers—and now the Orlando Magic, which he cofounded in 1987 and helped lead to the NBA finals in 1995 and 2009. Twenty-three of his teams have gone to the NBA playoffs and five have made the NBA finals. In 1996, Pat was named as one of the 50 most influential people in NBA history by a national publication.

Pat has been an integral part of NBA history, including bringing the NBA to Orlando. He has traded Pete Maravich as well as traded for Julius Erving, Moses Malone, and Penny Hardaway, and he has won four NBA draft lotteries, including back-to-back winners in 1992 and 1993. He also drafted Charles Barkley, Shaquille O'Neal, Maurice Cheeks, Andrew Toney, and Darryl Dawkins. He signed Billy Cunningham, Chuck Daly, and Matt Guokas to their first professional coaching contracts. Nineteen of his former players have become NBA head coaches, nine have become college head coaches, while seven have become assistant NBA coaches.